BOBBY FISCHER TEACHES CHESS

Here is the fastest, most efficient, most *enjoyable* book on chess ever compiled.

YOU

as the student start at the beginning and progressively develop your skills as you apply Bobby Fischer's principles and learn how to play Chess the Bobby Fischer way.

When you finish this [illegible] able to beat the greate[illegible] er known, *BUT* you w[illegible] than you were.

Bobby Fisch[illegible] player in the world, was born in [illegible] Illinois, in 1943. He was introduced to Chess and learned the moves when he was six years old. In his teens he achieved international prominence by winning every United States Chess competition for four years running without the loss of a game. He was the youngest International Grandmaster in Chess history. In the summer of 1972, Bobby Fischer of the United States will play Boris Spassky of the Soviet Union for the world's championship in Chess.

BY
Bobby Fischer
International Grandmaster

Stuart Margulies, Ph.D.
Educational Design, Inc.

Donn Mosenfelder
Educational Design, Inc.

Cover photo by Jerry Cooke, Sports Illustrated

ACKNOWLEDGMENTS

For some time we have been convinced that by merging the efforts of outstanding experts in Chess and in programmed instruction we could improve the Chess skills of a wide range of people. The coordinated efforts of many people were necessary to realize this aim. In particular, we would like to express our appreciation to: Leslie H. Ault (a former U.S. Intercollegiate Champion), who assisted with the original development of the programmed sequence and who served as general editor during the preparation for publication; Raymond Weinstein (an International Master who has represented the U S. in the Chess Olympics), who assisted with the original design; and Michael Valvo (a master-rated player who has played with the U.S. Student Team), who served as technical editor. We would also like to thank the professional staffs of Basic Systems, Inc., and Educational Design, Inc., for their significant contributions in the design, development testing, and production of the program.

BOBBY FISCHER TEACHES CHESS

A Bantam Book / published by arrangement with Xerox Learning Systems

PRINTING HISTORY

Xerox edition published January 1966
2nd printing .... June 1966
3rd printing ... December 1966

Bantam edition / May 1972

2nd printing ...... June 1972	*8th printing . September 1972*
3rd printing .... July 1972	*9th printing ... October 1972*
4th printing .... August 1972	*10th printing ... October 1972*
5th printing .... August 1972	*11th printing .... March 1973*
6th printing .. September 1972	*12th printing ...... May 1973*
7th printing .. September 1972	*13th printing . December 1975*

14th printing ... February 1977

For information address: Xerox Learning Systems, 600 Madison Avenue, New York, N.Y. 10022.

ISBN 0-553-10752-6

Published simultaneously in the United States and Canada

Bantam Books are published by Bantam Books, Inc. Its trademark, consisting of the words "Bantam Books" and the portrayal of a bantam, is registered in the United States Patent Office and in other countries. Marca Registrada. Bantam Books, Inc., 666 Fifth Avenue, New York, New York 10019.

PRINTED IN THE UNITED STATES OF AMERICA

0 9 8 7 6 5 4

CONTENTS

A WORD FROM BOBBY FISCHER

My book was written to help you play better Chess. It can help you even if you don't know Chess notation and only play casually every now and then. It can help you if you are more experienced and have begun to play in tournaments. It can also help you if you don't know how to play at all.

For the beginner, I have included an Introduction on the moves. After reading this Introduction, beginners will be able to go through the book easily. However, a little practice playing at this point—even a game or two—would help.

The book teaches the common mating positions and combinations. Since checkmating is the object of the game, I think it is the most basic thing to learn. The checkmate is the "knockout" of Chess. The book starts with one-move mates and then develops these ideas into mates of two, three, or four moves. You will be able to see these mates and apply them in your games.

Ordinarily, Chess books place you in a passive role. You are expected to study the material and remember it. My book presents material as a tutor would and requires you to actively use the new ideas immediately by answering questions. After answering each question, you simply turn the page to find the right answer and my explanation. In this way, you will absorb the material thoroughly.

Programmed instruction, the method used in this book, is a new concept in teaching. It has been used previously in industry and schools with excellent results.

You can learn quickly and retain the material far better than with ordinary textbooks or lectures. Even the beginner will remember what I teach him and be able to use it immediately.

The book will do two things for you. First, it will teach you to analyze Chess problems better. Second, it will teach you the themes to look for so that you can find the right move fairly quickly, sometimes in just a few seconds. There are lots of positions in the book to practice on. You will begin to recognize when mates are possible and how to pull them off. Just be sure to start at the beginning and work through the book. If you run into difficulties and can't work out an answer by yourself, turn the page to find my answer and explanation.

You can pick up the book whenever you have a chance, then break off and continue later. You can set your own pace in figuring out your moves and answering the questions. You don't need a chessboard and a set—only this book and a few minutes to spare now and then.

After you finish this book, you can buy a small but serviceable chessboard and set very inexpensively. Even a good tournament set costs only eight or ten dollars.

Chess games are being played everywhere—on benches and tables in the park, at Chess clubs, YMCA's, high schools, colleges, army posts, prisons. Even by mail. You shouldn't have any trouble in getting a game. I certainly hope that my book will help everyone to enjoy this wonderful game.

Bobby Fischer

THE PHENOMENAL BOBBY FISCHER

He was born Robert James Fischer on March 9, 1943, in Chicago, and grew up in Brooklyn. His sister, Joan, bought a Chess set when he was six, and together they learned the moves from the enclosed directions.

Bobby's development in Chess was unparalleled. By the time he was thirteen, he had achieved international prominence by winning what is generally known as the "Game of the Century." In 1957 he won the United States Chess Championship for the first time. He was fourteen. Bobby won or drew every single game in United States Chess competition for the next four years.

In the 1963–64 United States Chess Championship, Bobby achieved the unprecedented feat of winning all eleven games (without a single draw).

In the 1965 Capablanca Memorial Tournament, Bobby showed not only his great Chess ability but also his amazing stamina. Because of travel restrictions to Cuba, Bobby played all his opponents by teletype. This was undoubtedly one of his toughest tournaments.

In 1970 he began possibly the most famous drive in Chess history. He won seven straight games in international tournament play. Then, in May 1971, Bobby met Mark Taimanov, a Russian, in the challenge rounds of the World Championship.

He achieved the first shutout in the history of grandmaster play. The score was six games to none. He had won thirteen consecutive games. In the next round he beat Denmark's Bent Larsen by the same score! Nineteen games in a row. Bobby next met ex world champion Tigran Petrosian, a Russian, in Buenos Aires. If he beat Petrosian, Bobby would play Boris Spassky, another Russian, for the world title. Bobby won the first game stretching his winning streak to twenty. Then he caught a cold and lost a game. It was deadlocked for a short time until Bobby regained his momentum with the score at 2½ to 2½ (½ points are awarded for draws). Bobby ran the last four games to win 6½ to 2½ and begin a new winning streak.

Bobby plays Boris Spassky in mid-1972 for the World Championship. He may well end the decades-long Russian domination of the sport. As a German Chess expert told *Life* magazine, "No other master has such a terrific will to win. At the board he radiates danger, and even the strongest opponents tend to freeze, like rabbits when they smell a panther. Even his weaknesses are dangerous. As white, his opening is predictable—you can make plans against it—but so strong that your plans almost never work. In middle game his precision and invention are fabulous, and in the end game you simply cannot beat him."

ABOUT THE CO-AUTHORS

The co-authors of this book are Chess addicts, pioneers in the development of instructional techniques, and personal friends of long standing who have worked together on many projects.

Dr. Stuart Margulies, President of Ludi Education, a wholly owned subsidiary of Educational Design, Inc., has written a large number of instructional programs used in industry and the schools. His most famous contribution is the Effective Listening course, recently voted the outstanding programmed course in the country by a poll of experts in advanced learning techniques. Dr. Margulies is rated a Chess Master, and has tied for first place in the U.S. Amateur Chess Championships.

Donn Mosenfelder, co-founder and Editor-in-Chief of Educational Design, Inc., is one of the leading innovators in the field of programmed instruction. He has designed and written a large number of programmed courses, and has also pioneered in the development of new approaches to such varied instructional problems as on-the-job training, classroom management, and the evaluation of systems of instruction.

Five years ago, Dr. Margulies and Mr. Mosenfelder began to think of writing a new and truly different Chess book—a book that would systematically develop a student's ability to recognize and exploit some of the infinite variations on basic tactical and strategic themes that actually occur in Chess play. But to do this they needed the insights that only a truly great Chess mind could provide—they needed a collaborator who was both a great player and a great theorist, who could develop and evaluate positions, refine themes, and contribute insights from actual games of Grand Master caliber.

They found such a collaborator in Bobby Fischer.

This book is the result. It teaches faster, more efficiently, and more enjoyably than conventional methods. You, the student, progressively develop your skills as you learn to apply Bobby's principles. You will not be able to beat Bobby Fischer after you take this course, but one thing is guaranteed: you will become a far better Chess player than you were. The co-authors did.

INTRODUCTION: HOW TO PLAY CHESS

This section is optional. It is intended for readers who do not know how to play Chess or for those who need to review the rules before starting the main part of this book.

If you are already familiar with the moves, turn to page 15.

A DESCRIPTION OF THE BOARD AND THE PIECES

Chess is played by two players who move by turns. Play takes place on a chessboard that contains 64 squares, i.e., eight rows of eight squares. The squares are alternately colored white and black. The board should be arranged in such a way that each player has a white square in the corner at his right.

The Chessboard.

The chess pieces are colored light and dark, and are designated as White and Black. Each side starts off with sixteen chessmen:

White		Black
♔	1 King	♚
♕	1 Queen	♛
♖	2 Rooks	♜
♗	2 Bishops	♝
♘	2 Knights	♞
♙	8 Pawns	♟

The starting arrangement of the pieces on the board, looking from the White side:

Black

White

Note that the Queen starts from the square of its own color and that the King is placed next to its Queen. (Opposing Kings and Queens face each other.)

White always moves first.

MOVING AND CAPTURING

A move is the transfer of a chess piece from one square to another. A capture is the removal of an opposing piece from the board; it is accomplished by actually removing the piece from its square and replacing it with the capturing piece. (You cannot capture your own piece.)

Powers of the Pieces

The King can move or capture one square in any direction.

The King can move to any square marked with an x.

The King cannot move to squares where it may be captured by enemy pieces; nor can the King move to squares already occupied by its own pieces. The King can capture an enemy piece within its moving range by removing the enemy piece from the board and by placing itself on the square occupied by the removed piece.

The King can capture the Pawn as shown:

The Queen can move or capture as far as it wants in any direction—horizontally, vertically, or diagonally—unless it is obstructed by a piece belonging to either side.

The Queen can move to any square marked with an x.

Here, too, the Queen can move to any square marked with an x, but it cannot move to the square occupied by its own Rook or the squares that lie beyond the Rook.

The Queen can move to any square marked with an x, or it can capture the Black Bishop by removing it from the board and placing itself on the square occupied by the Bishop. But, it cannot move to the squares that lie beyond the Bishop.

The Rook can move or capture horizontally or vertically like the Queen, but lacks the power to move diagonally.

The Rook can move to any square marked with an x.

The Rook also captures by removing the enemy piece and occupying its square.

The Bishop is limited to diagonal moves or captures. It cannot move horizontally or vertically.

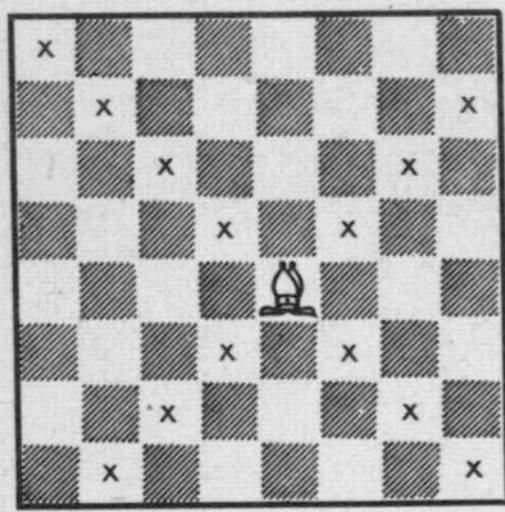

The Bishop's moves.

Since the Bishop can only move diagonally, it is confined to squares of the same color throughout the game. The Bishop can capture any enemy piece within its moving range.

The Knight moves differently from any other piece. Its crooked move often confuses beginners, so I will describe it in three ways:

The Knight moves to squares reached by going two squares vertically or horizontally, and one square to the left or right.

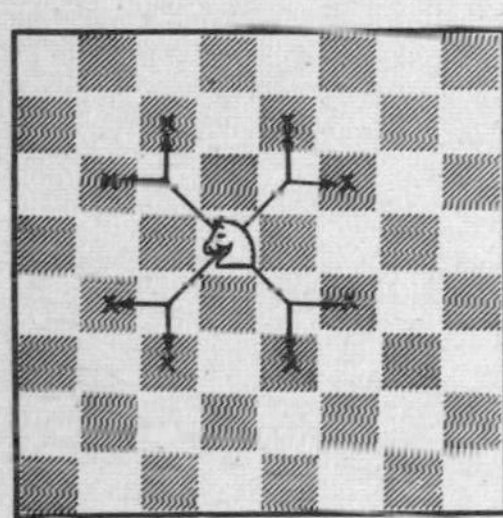

The Knight moves to squares reached by going one square diagonally and then one square horizontally or vertically in roughly the same direction.

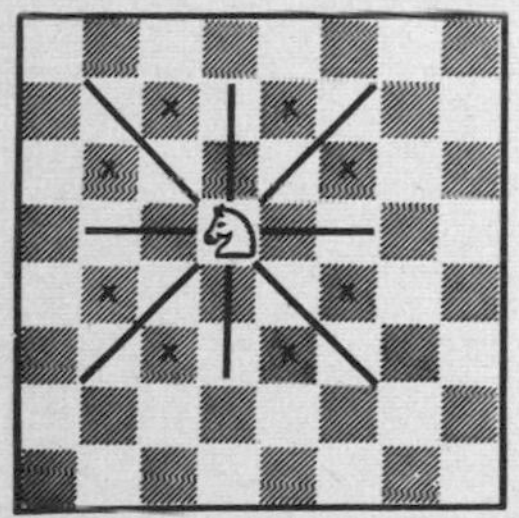

The Knight moves to the eight nearby squares which are not in a horizontal, vertical, or diagonal straight line from the square it occupies.

Note that the Knight always lands on a square of a different color from the one it started on.

The Knight is the only piece that can jump over other pieces (either its own or the enemy's) in the course of its move.

For example, in the initial position, White could start with any of four Knight moves, as shown.

The Knight captures in the same way that it moves: by replacing the enemy piece on the square to which it moves.

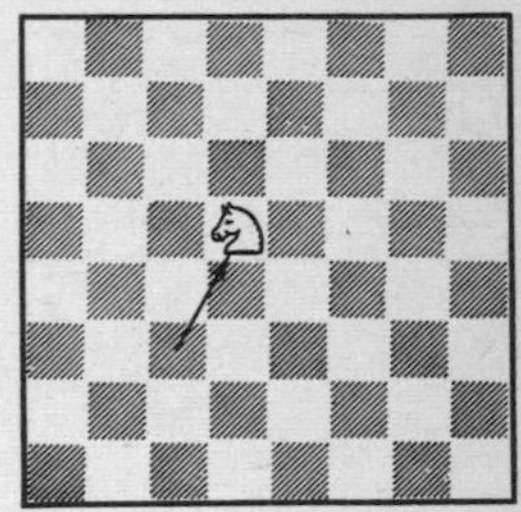

The Pawn, unlike the other pieces, moves in one fashion and captures in another. Also, it can only advance, never retreat. The Pawn moves forward—never backward—one square at a time, as shown:

However, when the Pawn is on its original square, it has the option of advancing one or two squares on its first move.

The Pawn can move to square A or square B.

The Pawn captures diagonally forward to the left or right, as shown:

How the Pawn captures.

In the position shown below, the White Pawn on the left can capture the Knight; however, it cannot move one square ahead, since it is blocked by the Black Bishop. Neither Pawn on the right can move since each blocks the other.

Remember that the Pawn, like the other pieces, replaces the piece it captures.

Position before the Pawn captures.

After the Pawn captures. The Pawn then proceeds as shown by the broken line, unless it changes files (the vertical rows) when making another capture.

Special Moves

Castling is a move that allows you to place your King on a square that is reasonably safe from enemy attack. It is the only move that involves a move of two pieces on a player's turn. Castling is accomplished by the King and either Rook as shown below:

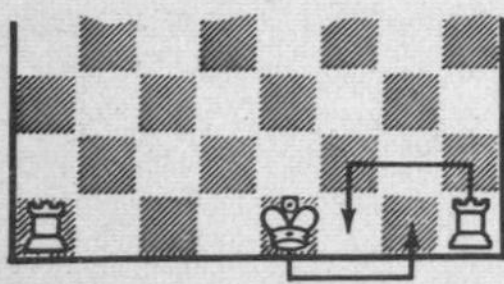

Position before castling on the King's side of the board.

After castling "King-side."

Position before castling on the Queen's side of the board.

After castling "Queen-side."

Black castles as shown:

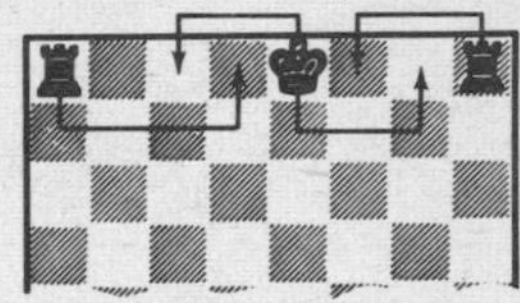

Note: The King is moved two squares toward the Rook he intends to castle with, then the Rook is placed on the other side of the King.

Castling may not be played when:

1) The King is in check, i.e., under enemy attack.
2) Either the King or Rook involved has previously moved.
3) Pieces (either side) are between the King and the Rook.
4) Squares passed over or landed on by the King are under enemy attack.

Pawn Promotion: When a Pawn reaches the eighth rank (the enemy's back rank) it is promoted to a Queen, Rook, Bishop, or Knight of its own color, according to the player's choice.

Capturing En Passant (in passing): This special capturing power of a Pawn applies only to the capture of a Pawn by a Pawn, in a specific type of situation. That situation occurs when a Pawn on the second rank (horizontal row) uses its option to advance two squares on its first move and bypasses an enemy Pawn as shown here.

White moves.

Now it is Black's move.

Black now has the option of capturing the White Pawn as if it had advanced one square.

Before Black captures en passant.

After Black captures en passant.

If the bypassed Pawn does not exercise its option of capturing en passant at once, it cannot do so later on in the game.

RELATIVE VALUES OF PIECES

Numerically, the relative values of the various pieces can be expressed as follows: Pawn = 1; Knight = 3; Bishop = 3.25; Rook = 5; Queen = 9; King = Infinity (if you lose the King, you lose the game).

NOTE: You may now start the program on page 15. If you are new to Chess, you may find that you need to review some of the rules as you are working through the first part of the program. If you do, you may turn back here and "brush up" before continuing.

Chapter 1

ELEMENTS OF CHECKMATE

1

HOW TO USE THIS BOOK

In preparing this book, I did not want to write just an ordinary Chess book—so I used a new method called programmed instruction. Instead of merely presenting information that you have to try to understand, this book, called a program, actively teaches the material it contains.

A program consists of a series of small informational steps called frames. Each frame presents information and usually requires a written response from you, the learner. Some frames will ask you to check a "yes" or "no" answer, others will ask you to write a sentence of explanation, and most will ask you to indicate a correct move by drawing an arrow on a diagram. My answer to each frame appears in the answer box at the top of the next right-hand page. This allows you to compare your answer with mine after you've had a chance to work out your own response. You are not asked questions about information that hasn't been taught in the program. You will notice that each frame builds on positions previously presented and prepares for positions to follow.

When you reach the last page of this book, turn the book around and continue working on the right-hand pages.

When you finish the book, you will find that you can "finish off" your opponent with mating combinations you never would have seen before.

You may now turn to frame number 2 on the next right-hand page. I hope you will enjoy learning Chess from BOBBY FISCHER TEACHES CHESS.

2

DIAGRAMS

Diagrams may seem puzzling at first, but once you know what each symbol stands for they are very simple. Let's review the pieces and their symbols one by one:

King	Queen	Rook
symbol ♔	symbol ♕	symbol ♖

Bishop	Knight	Pawn
symbol ♗	symbol ♘	symbol ♙

(continued)

2 (continued)

The initial position in diagram form:

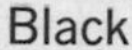

Black Pawns move in this direction.

White Pawns move in this direction

White

In diagrams, the White side of the board is always placed on the bottom.

3

TO THE EXPERIENCED PLAYER

If you have played Chess several times and are confident that you understand checkmate, you may now turn to frame 39 on page 60 and begin the program. You should turn back to frame 5 if you find frame 39, or any of the frames immediately following it, difficult to answer.

If you haven't played much Chess, you should turn to the next frame and begin.

4

THE OBJECT OF CHESS

The object of Chess is to attack the enemy King in such a way that it cannot escape capture. Once this is done the King is "checkmated" and the game is terminated. Therefore, whenever a King is under attack ("check"), it must escape that attack before the game can go on.

Consider the following position:

Diagram A

Black is in check.

The White Rook is checking the Black King. There are three ways of escaping check:

1) Capturing the checking piece (Bishop: arrow 1).
2) Interposing a piece between the King and the checking piece (Rook: arrow 2).
3) Fleeing to a square where the King will not be in check (arrow 3).

(continued)

4 (continued)

Remember, if a King is in check and has no way of escaping, then that King is "checkmated."

Consider this position:

Diagram B

Checkmate!

Here the checking piece (Queen) can't be captured because it is protected by the Rook. Black has no possible interpositions and all the potential fleeing squares (A, B, C, D) are attacked by the White Queen. Black is in check and has no means of escaping: Black is checkmated. The game is over.

Compare the position above with the one that follows:

Diagram C

(Black to move.)

(What move can Black make?)

In diagram B, Black is in check and has no moves to escape from check. But in diagram C, Black is not in check; any move with his King would put his King in check, <u>and</u> his Pawn is blocked. Black has no legal move. This situation is known as "stalemate" and the game is drawn.

5

Let's see how checkmate is accomplished and how your opponent might escape it.

Observe the difference between the two positions in each of the groups below:

A1. White has just moved his Rook down, giving check. But the Black King can capture the checking White Rook. Black is saved.

A2. In this slightly different position, the attacked King cannot capture the White Rook. As a matter of fact, Black has no defense; he is checkmated. The game is over.

5 (continued)

B1. The White Queen has cornered Black's King, but Black's King can capture the checking White Queen.

B2 The checking White Queen is protected by the Bishop. The Black King cannot capture. Black is checkmated.

C1. Again, the Black King can capture the attacking Queen.

C2. Here the Queen, protected by a Rook, has checkmated Black.

NOW TURN THE PAGE AND CONTINUE WITH FRAME 6

White's Queen checked on the back rank, and Black resigned. Black's only chance would be to play Rook-takes-Queen. (If the Knight interposes, the Pawn takes the Knight and promotes to a Queen, with check and mate on the next move.) The capture allows the White Bishop to check, whereupon Black must give up his Queen and Rook to prevent mate: the Rook interposes; Bishop-takes-Rook-check; Queen-takes-Bishop; and Pawn-takes-Queen. Here is the resulting position:

Benko

Fischer

White has a Rook and two Pawns for a Knight; besides this material advantage, he will soon be able to promote one of his advanced Pawns.

Congratulations! You have just completed the program.

I sincerely hope that my book will help you play better Chess. It will be a good sign if you can now beat some of your old opponents who have not taken the program.

Bobby Fischer

6

Observe this position; then decide whether the Black King can capture the checking White piece.

The White Queen is giving check. The Black King:

☐ can capture

☐ cannot capture

FOR THE CORRECT ANSWER TURN TO THE NEXT PAGE

275

yes

(I took the Pawn, giving check. If Black had then captured my Queen, I would have mated him with my Knight. Or if he had moved his King, I would have mated with Queen-takes-Pawn [next to the King]. Black resigned.)

A FINAL WORD

As one last illustration of the employment of the mating themes taught in this program, here is the finish of a game that helped me retain my title in the most recent U.S. Championship (December, 1965). In the position diagrammed below, I (White) forced my opponent's resignation with one crushing move. You might see if you can find that move—although I won't require you to do so. It's a difficult one since Black can escape checkmate, but . . .

Benko

Fischer

(continued)

6

cannot capture
(NOTE: The Queen is protected by the Bishop; therefore the King cannot capture. In fact, the King has no safe place to move to. So Black is checkmated.)

7

Again, observe the position; then decide whether the Black King can capture the checking White piece.

The White Queen is giving check. The Black King:

- ☐ can capture
- ☐ cannot capture

FOR THE CORRECT ANSWER TURN TO THE NEXT PAGE

274

no
(The Black Bishop can interpose safely.)

275

From Fischer-Benko, 1962:

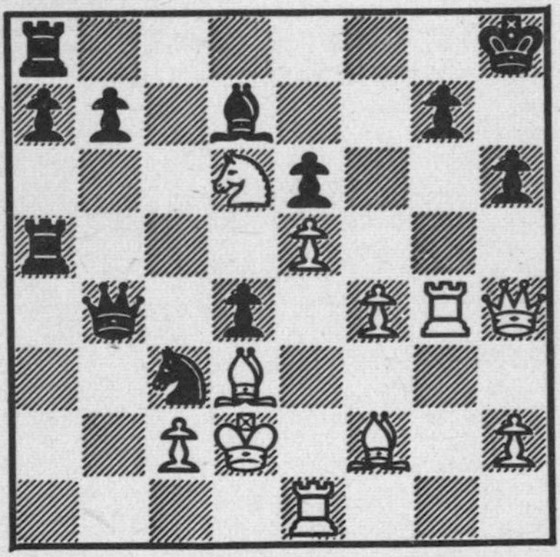

Can White mate?

☐ yes
☐ no

7

can capture
(NOTE: The Bishop is not protecting the Queen.)

8

Black King:

- ☐ can capture checking White Rook
- ☐ cannot capture checking White Rook

273

yes

(Then the White Rook at the lower left checks, with mate on the next move.)

274

Can White mate?

☐ yes

☐ no

If he can, draw an arrow to show his first move.

8

can capture checking White Rook

9

Black King:

- ☐ can capture checking White Rook
- ☐ cannot capture checking White Rook

272

yes

(The Knight is drawn away to capture the Queen; then White sends his Rook down, giving check, and leaving Black with one useless interposition before checkmate.)

273

Does White mate?

☐ yes

☐ no

If "yes," draw an arrow showing his first move.

9

cannot capture checking White Rook
(The Rook is protected by the Knight.)

10

Black King:

- ☐ can capture checking White Rook
- ☐ cannot capture checking White Rook

271

yes

(From Souza-Mendes vs. Fischer [Black], Argentina, 1959.)

272

Does White mate?

☐ yes

☐ no

If "yes," show the correct move by an arrow.

10

can capture checking White Rook

11

Black King:

- ☐ can capture checking White Rook
- ☐ cannot capture checking White Rook

270

no
(If Queen-takes-Pawn-check, the Bishop takes the Queen and Black says "Thank you!")

271

Here's a finish from one of my games:

Can Black mate?

☐ yes
☐ no

If he can, draw an arrow showing the correct move.

11

cannot capture checking White Rook
(Black is "mated"—or checkmated. Remember, the King can only move one square, so the Rook is beyond the Black King's reach.)

12

Sometimes the Black King can escape from check by fleeing to a "flight" square.
Observe the difference between the two positions in each of the groups below:

A1. The Black King can flee (as shown by arrow) from a check by the White Knight.

A2. In this slightly different position Black's King, in check, has no flight squares and no other defense—he is mated. We call this a "smothered" mate because the Black King, hemmed in by its own pieces, has no place to move when checked by the Knight.

(continued)

269

yes

(This one is tricky—it looks like it doesn't work: Black's Rook-takes-Rook, Rook-takes-Rook, Bishop-takes-Rook but now . . . White mates by moving his Queen to square X.)

270

Does White mate?

- ☐ yes
- ☐ no

If "yes," show his first move with an arrow.

12 (continued)

B1. The White Queen has checked, but Black's King can flee to the square indicated.

B2. Here White's Queen not only checks, but also covers the enemy King's flight square. Black has no place to flee safely, so he is mated.

C1. The White Rook checks. Black's King flees as indicated.

C2. White's Bishop covers the flight square. Therefore, Black is mated.

TURN THE PAGE AND CONTINUE WITH FRAME 13

268

yes

(On Rook-takes-Queen, White advances his Rook to the back rank, giving checkmate.)

269

Does White mate?

☐ yes

☐ no

If "yes," show his correct move with an arrow.

12

NO ANSWER REQUIRED

13

Now you decide what Black can do in this position.

Black King:

- ☐ can capture its attacker
- ☐ can flee
- ☐ can do neither

267

no
(On Queen-checks, Black interposes with his Queen—but if he plays Rook-takes-Queen, White mates.)

268

Can White mate?

- ☐ yes
- ☐ no

If he can, draw an arrow showing his first move.

13

can do neither
(Black is mated. The Bishops team up powerfully here.)

14

Again, observe the position and decide what the Black King can do.

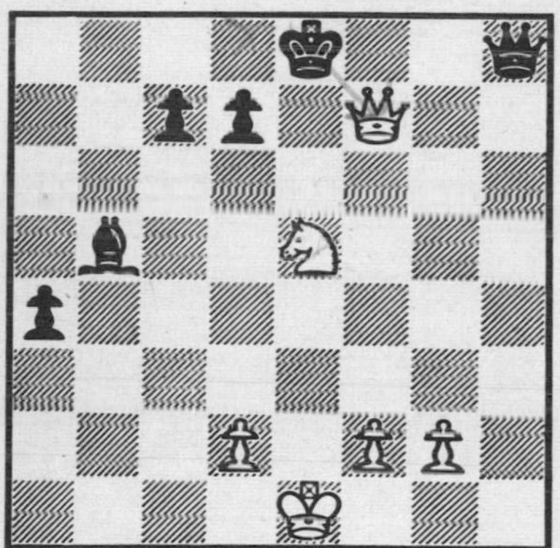

Black King:

- ☐ can capture attacker
- ☐ can flee
- ☐ can do neither

266

yes

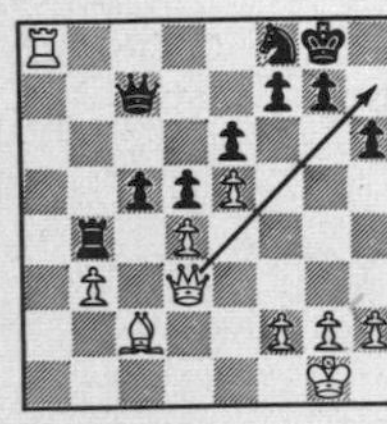

267

Can White mate?

☐ yes

☐ no

If he can, show the correct move with an arrow.

14

can flee
(One square to your left. Work it out.)

15

Black King:

☐ can capture attacker
☐ can flee
☐ can do neither

265

yes

266

Does White mate?

☐ yes

☐ no

If "yes," draw an arrow showing his move.

15

can do neither
(White's Pawn stops Black's King from fleeing.)

16

Black King:

- ☐ can capture attacker
- ☐ can flee
- ☐ can do neither

264

yes

(Next, White plays Queen-checks, leading to mate. Note that the escape square at X is covered by White's Bishop. This works even if Black's Queen interposes on Black's first move from the position shown. Work it out!)

265

Does White mate?

☐ yes

☐ no

If "yes," draw an arrow to show his move.

16

can capture attacker

17

Here the lowly Pawn is giving check:

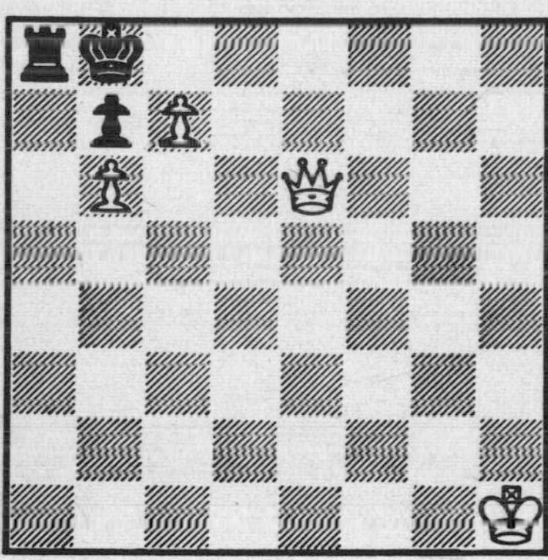

Black King:

- ☐ can capture attacker
- ☐ can flee
- ☐ can do neither

263

yes

264

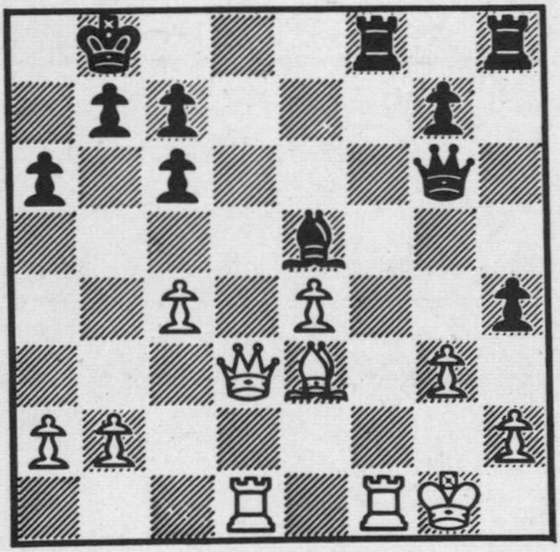

Can White mate?

☐ yes

☐ no

If he can, draw an arrow to show the correct move.

17

can do neither
(Black is mated.)

18

Black King:

☐ can capture attacker
☐ can flee
☐ can do neither

262

yes

(After the Knight checks, the Pawn takes the Knight, Rook [on the bottom rank] moves two squares to the left, giving check and driving the King into the corner, thereby enabling White to play Queen-takes-Rook-mate.)

263

Does White mate?

☐ yes

☐ no

If "yes," show his first move with an arrow.

18

can do neither
(Checking Rook is protected by Queen. Black is mated.)

19

Draw an arrow to show how I (Black) mated Paul Keres in this position.

Fischer

Keres

261

yes

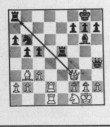

(After Knight-takes-Queen, White plays Rook down-check.)

262

Does White mate?

☐ yes

☐ no

If "yes," show his first move with an arrow.

19

Fischer

Keres

NOTE: This mate actually happened! The position is taken from our game in the 1959 Bled Tournament (Yugoslavia). Since 1938 Keres has been considered one of the very top players in the world.

20

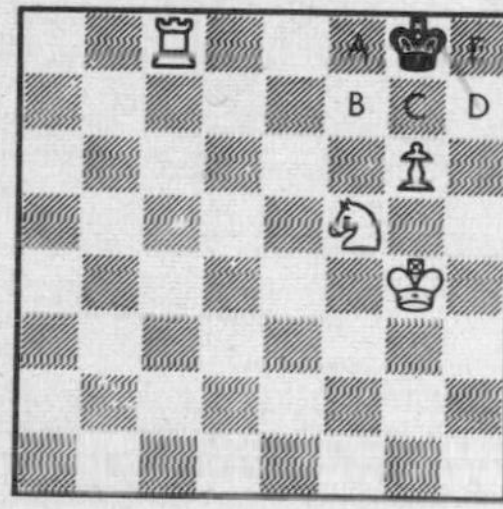

White's Rook has checked. The Black King, having no flight square, is mated.

Note the lettered squares, then identify the White piece that guards each of them. (For example, if the Black King were to move to square A, which White piece could capture it?) I'll do the first one to give you the idea.

ROOK guards square A
__________ guards square B
__________ guards square C
__________ guards square D
__________ guards square E

260

no

261

Can White mate?

☐ yes

☐ no

If he can, draw an arrow to show his first move.

20

Pawn (guards square B)
Knight (guards square C)
Pawn (guards square D)
Rook (guards square E)

21

Now try this one:

Identify the White piece that guards each square:

______________ guards square A
______________ guards square B
______________ guards square C
______________ guards square D
______________ guards square E

By the way, which White piece is giving check?

____

259

no
(Black's back rank is adequately protected.)

260

Does White mate?

☐ yes
☐ no

If "yes," show his first move with an arrow.

21

Queen (guards square A)
Bishop (guards square B)
Knight (guards square C)
King (guards square D)
Pawn (guards square E)
No White piece is giving check.

(Black has no possible move; therefore, the game is a stalemate, or draw.)

22

Observe this position; then draw an arrow to show White's mating move:

258

yes

(On King-takes-Rook, the Queen move to square X is checkmate.)

259

Can White mate?

☐ yes

☐ no

If he can, show the first move by an arrow.

22

(This was taken from my game with Bent Larsen [Black] in the 1958 Interzonal Tournament, in Portoroz, Yugoslavia.)

23

Black is in check again

Draw an arrow pointing to the one square to which Black can flee:

257

no
(Black has enough pieces protecting the crucial square on his back rank.)

258

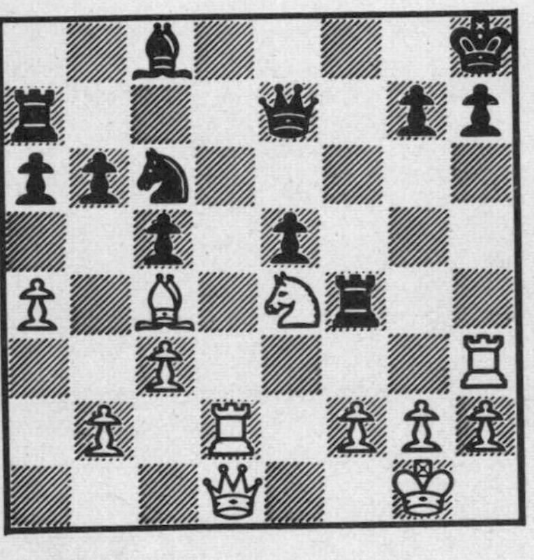

Can White mate?

- ☐ yes
- ☐ no

If "yes," draw an arrow showing his first move.

23

24

Again, draw an arrow to show Black's flight square:

256

yes

(Queen-takes-Pawn-checkmate!)

257

Can White mate?

- ☐ yes
- ☐ no

If he can, draw an arrow indicating the first move.

24

25

Here's a common position in which Black appears to be checkmated. Actually he can escape, but in a slightly different way from what you've been accustomed to.

Draw an arrow on the diagram to show how Black's King gets out of check:

255

yes

(White mates: Queen-takes-Rook-check; King-takes-Queen; Rook to square X-check; Queen interposes; Rook-takes-Queen-mate.)

256

Does White mate?

☐ yes

☐ no

If "yes," show his first move with an arrow.

25

(Black has only one place to go, and it just happens that a White Rook is occupying that square. The King saves himself by capturing the Rook—so much the better.)

26

Can White save himself by playing King-takes-Rook in this position?

- ☐ yes
- ☐ no (checkmate)

254

yes

(When Black recaptures the Rook, White checks on the back rank; Knight interposes. White then mates by driving the King away: the Queen or Bishop checks on square K, followed by Queen-takes-Knight-mate.)

255

Can White mate?

☐ yes

☐ no

If White can mate, show his first move with an arrow.

26

no (checkmate)
(In this case the Queen, which is giving check, also protects the Rook. White is checkmated.)

27

Remember that one King can help trap the other. In fact, in the later stages of the game when most of the pieces have been traded off, the King can be a very valuable offensive piece—and not one that you have to hide away in the corner.
Observe the positions below:

A

B

Black is checkmated in:

- ☐ position A only
- ☐ position B only
- ☐ both positions
- ☐ neither position

253

no
(Here when White drives the King one square to the left, the King will have access to a fleeing square, preventing the back-rank mate.)

254

Can White mate?

☐ yes
☐ no

If White can mate, draw an arrow to show his first move.

27

position A only
(Note that in position A the White King hems in Black's King while the Rook gives check. This is a common type of mate. In position B, Black has a fleeing square that gets him safely out of check. Look again for it if you didn't notice it.)

28

Now that you have the idea, observe this position:

Is Black checkmated?

☐ yes
☐ no

252

yes

(White first drives the King into the corner, then sacrifices his Queen in order to force mate on the back rank.)

253

Does White mate?

☐ yes

☐ no

If "yes," draw an arrow to show his first move.

28

yes
(The Queen gives check and covers all the fleeing squares, while White's King protects the Queen from capture.)

29

Sometimes Black can avoid check or mate by capturing with a piece other than his King.

Observe the difference between the two positions in each group below:

A1. White's Queen, protected by the Rook, has mated.

A2. The same position, except for the Black Bishop, which can capture the attacker.

(continued)

251

yes

(After Black plays King-takes-Queen, White moves his Rook over, giving check. Black has only the useless interposition with his Bishop and is then mated by the Rook.)

252

Can White mate?

☐ yes
☐ no

If he can, draw an arrow to show his first move.

29 (continued)

B1. White's Queen, protected by Bishop, mates.

B2. But here the Black Knight can capture the attacker.

C1. The White Rook mates. The Bishop prevents the Black Rook from capturing the White Rook and thereby saving the game.

C2. With the Black Bishop out of the way, Black's Rook captures White's Rook.

TURN THE PAGE AND CONTINUE WITH FRAME 30

250

no

251

Can White mate?

☐ yes

☐ no

If he can, draw an arrow to show his move.

29

NO ANSWER REQUIRED

30

Observe the following position; then determine Black's defense, if any.

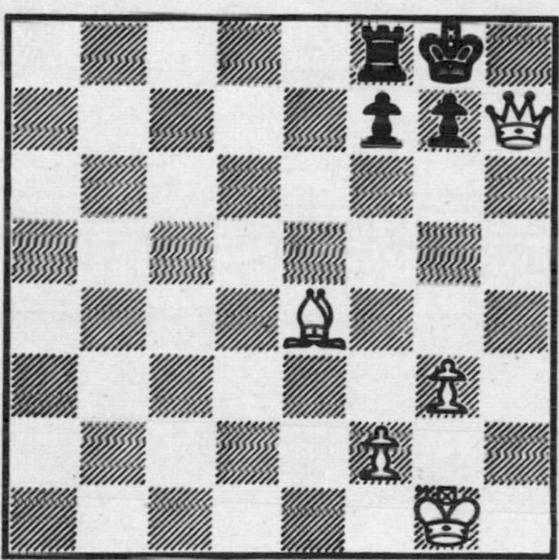

What is Black's defense?

- ☐ King-takes-Queen
- ☐ King flees
- ☐ other piece-takes-Queen
- ☐ no defense: checkmate

249

no
(Black should take White's Queen and then interpose with his Bishop.)

250

Does White mate?

☐ yes
☐ no

If "yes," draw an arrow showing his first move.

30

no defense: checkmate

31

Check Black's defensive move:

☐ King-takes-Rook
☐ King flees
☐ other piece-takes-Rook
☐ no defense: checkmate

248

yes

249

Can White mate?

- ☐ yes
- ☐ no

If he can mate, show his first move with an arrow.

31

other piece-takes-Rook
(In this case the Knight is the capturing piece.)

32

What does Black play?

- ☐ King-takes-Rook
- ☐ King flees
- ☐ other piece-takes-Rook
- ☐ no defense: checkmate

247

yes

248

Does White mate?

☐ yes

☐ no

If "yes," draw an arrow to show his move.

32

King-takes-Rook

33

What is Black's defense?

- ☐ King-takes-Queen
- ☐ King flees
- ☐ other piece-takes-Queen
- ☐ no defense: checkmate

246

no
(After Rook-takes-Rook-check, Bishop-takes-Rook, the remaining White Rook checks and Black interposes with his Rook.)

247

Can White mate?

☐ yes

☐ no

If he can mate, draw an arrow to show his move.

33

King flees

34

What is Black's saving move in this example?

- ☐ King-takes-Bishop
- ☐ King flees
- ☐ other piece-takes-Bishop
- ☐ no defense: checkmate

245

yes

(The Pawn is pinned and cannot take the Queen, so Black is mated.)

246

Can White mate?

☐ yes

☐ no

Don't forget to draw an arrow showing White's key first move, if any.

34

King flees

35

What can Black do to escape check?

- ☐ King-takes-Knight
- ☐ King flees
- ☐ other piece-takes-Knight
- ☐ no defense: checkmate

44

es

245

Can White mate?

☐ yes

☐ no

f "yes," draw an arrow to show his first move.

35

other piece-takes-Knight
(In this case, the Pawn saves Black by capturing the checking White Knight.)

36

Another way for Black to escape check is to "interpose" one of his pieces between the checking piece and his King.
Observe the following positions:

A. White's Rook has checked. Black has no defense and is mated.

B. But in this similar position, Black's Rook prevents mate by <u>interposing</u> (as shown by arrow).

(continued)

243

NO ANSWER REQUIRED

244

Can White mate?

☐ yes

☐ no

If he can mate, draw an arrow to show his key first move.

36 (continued)

C. Here Black's Bishop interposes, defending against mate by the White Rook.

D. This time the Black Knight interposes.

NOW TURN THE PAGE AND CONTINUE WITH FRAME 37

242

NO ANSWER REQUIRED

243

CRITERION POSITIONS

Now you're ready to try your skill at sorting out all of the concepts you've learned in a series of complex positions. Some of these positions are difficult. You'll have to decide in each case whether or not White can mate. In some of the positions, he cannot. Wherever there is a mate, draw an arrow to show the key first move for White.

NOW TURN THE PAGE AND CONTINUE WITH FRAME 244

36

NO ANSWER REQUIRED

37

In this position, the White Rook is checking:

Which Black piece can defend against the check?

____

What does that Black piece do?

- ☐ captures
- ☐ interposes

242 (continued)

And remember about pins against the King:

D. Mate: the pinned piece cannot capture.

E. The White Rook cannot mate because of the pin.

F. Pinned White Rook supports White Queen—checkmate.

NOW TURN THE PAGE AND CONTINUE WITH FRAME 243

37

the Knight

interposes

38

Which Black piece can defend against this check?

____

What does that Black piece do?

- ☐ captures
- ☐ interposes

242

Remember the three ways to get out of check:

A. Interposition.

B. Capturing a checking piece.

C. King flees.

(continued)

38

Pawn

captures (the Queen)

39

In this and the next few frames you will be shown various positions: in some Black is mated; in others he can defend by capturing the White attacker, moving his King, or interposing. You will be asked to determine Black's defense, if any exists.

Is Black mated by White's Bishop?

☐ yes

☐ no

If not, draw an arrow on the diagram to show Black's defense.

241

THE DEFENSES

The following positions review the defenses against various attacks:

A. Black's Queen should capture. (If the Black Rook captures, White would mate.)

B. Black's Rook should capture. (If the King captures, White would mate.)

C. Black's Queen should interpose. (If the Black Rook takes White's Queen, White would mate.)

D. White Queen sacrifice fails. (Black's Rook takes Queen; White Rook checks; Black Rook interposes; and now the check by White Bishop does no good.)

39

no
(Black is not mated; the Rook interposes, as shown.)

40

Is Black mated?

☐ yes
☐ no

If not, draw an arrow to show his defense.

240 (continued)

M. Another Queen sacrifice variation. (Black Queen captures; Rook at far right checks; Black Queen interposes; Rook takes Queen, giving mate.)

N. Mating a hemmed-in King. (King must capture; White Rook mates.)

O. Hemming in the King. (The Black King must move into the corner, allowing White to sacrifice his Queen and mate with his Rook.)

P. Hemming in the King: a variation. (Black's Pawn must capture, allowing White's Rook to mate.)

NOW TURN THE PAGE AND CONTINUE WITH FRAME 241

40

no
(King flees as shown.)

41

Observe the board carefully. This is a tricky one.

Is Black mated?

☐ yes
☐ no

If not, draw an arrow to show his defense.

240 (continued)

I. The Rook drives the King away (allowing Queen-takes-Rook-mate).

J. White checks with his Knight, in an attempt to drive the Black King into the corner and mate with Queen-takes-Queen. Black stalls by playing Pawn-takes-Knight, but then White checks with his Rook (three squares to left) and White mates with Queen-takes-Queen.

K. A Queen sacrifice. (After Black's Queen captures, it will be pinned; the White Rook can then mate.)

L. Queen sacrifice. (Black's Rook captures; White's Rook checks; Black's Rook interposes; Whites Bishop drives the King into the corner. Then White mates with Rook-takes Rook.)

41

yes
(You have to watch those Knights!)

42

Here's another tricky one:

The position is:

☐ checkmate
☐ not checkmate

If you answer "not checkmate," draw an arrow to show Black's defense.

240 (continued)

E. Drawing away a defender. (The Knight must capture, allowing White's other Rook to mate.)

F. Driving away the enemy King. (After Black's King moves, White can mate on the back rank.)

G. The Bishop drives away the King. (The Bishop takes off the Pawn, giving check. Black can't play King-takes-Bishop because the White Queen protects the Bishop; nor can he play Queen-takes-Bishop since the White Queen pins the Black Queen. So, the King must retreat into the corner. Then Queen-takes-Queen is mate.)

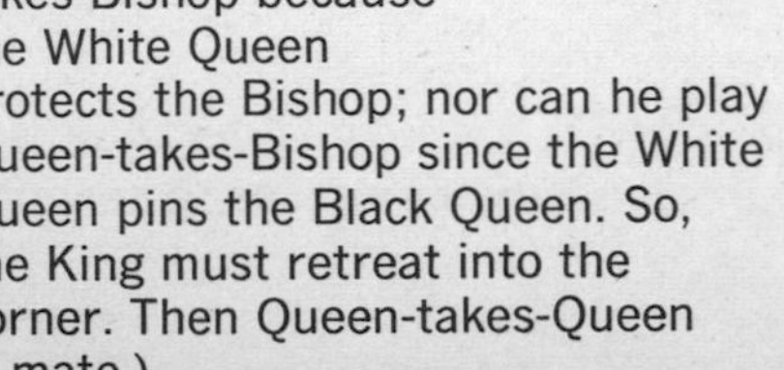

H. The Knight drives the King into the corner (allowing Rook-takes-Rook-mate).

(continued)

42

not checkmate
(Queen takes Queen, as shown.)

43

You will now see more complex positions that require careful consideration of every piece on the board.

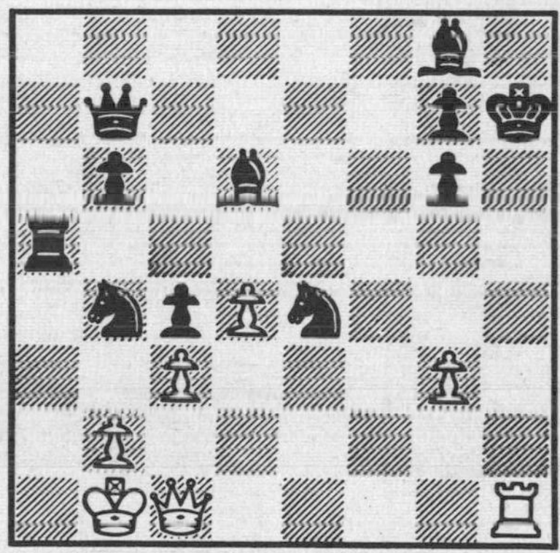

Which Black piece can defend against mate?

____

How does this piece defend?

- ☐ by capturing attacker
- ☐ by interposing

240

MATING THEMES

Observe the following positions, which review the various types of mating themes and their variations:

A. An elementary back-rank mate. (Black's interpositions are useless.)

B. A back-rank combination. (It's three against two and a back-rank mate.)

C. Eliminating a back-rank defender. (After Black's Queen captures, White's Rooks can mate.)

D. Eliminating a back-rank defender. (Black's King recaptures; White's Queen mates on the back rank, since it also blocks escape square A.)

(continued)

43

the Rook

by interposing
(You have to watch all of the pieces on the board and observe how they affect the position.)

44

Here's a position from one of my games in which I was Black.

Assume White's Pawn captures the Black Knight. Draw an arrow to show how I would then mate in one move:

Fischer

Gligorich

Chapter 6

FINAL REVIEW

The criterion positions at the end of this chapter will test your understanding of all the themes and variations you have learned.

First, however, let us summarize these themes and variations. You have learned the basic elements of checkmate, the back-rank mates and defenses, displacing themes, and an assortment of sacrificial combinations. The following diagrams illustrate these concepts in their basic form.

I have removed all the window dressing, leaving just the basic elements.

TURN THE PAGE AND CONTINUE WITH FRAME 240

44 After White's Pawn takes Knight, Queen mates as shown:

Fischer

Gligorich

NOTE: This position is from my game with Gligorich in Bled, Yugoslavia (1961). Gligorich has been Yugoslavian Champion many times. He has qualified for the Candidates Tournament for the World Championship three times.

Actually, my opponent made a different move (Knight-takes-Bishop), and after some complicated play the game was eventually drawn.

45

Draw an arrow to show Black's defense against checkmate:

This won a Rook, and Black soon resigned. Note that Black would still have remained a Rook "down" if he had played Queen-takes-Queen, giving check. How? Rook would have interposed! (The Rook would have exposed the Bishop check—again!—and when Black had replied to the check, I would have captured his Queen.)

THIS IS THE END OF CHAPTER 5
NOW TURN THE PAGE AND GO ON TO CHAPTER 6

45

(Remember, watch the whole board!)

46

Observe the board carefully:

Can White's Rook mate by capturing the Pawn, as shown?

☐ yes
☐ no

If Sherwin had then moved his king into the corner, Rook-takes-Rook would have been mate! Or, if the Rook interposes, the Rook on the left would mate Black. Taking my Bishop with his Queen wouldn't have helped because I would have played Rook-takes-Rook-check first and then (!) Pawn-takes-Black Queen. (See Diagram D below.)

Sherwin

Fischer

Diagram D (variation)
Rook-check; then Pawn-captures-Black Queen.

This would have left me with enough material advantage to win: Rook and Pawn against Knight.

Sherwin tried to make the best of a bad bargain (from Diagram B) by moving his Pawn up next to his Queen, creating an escape square for his King. Now I played Queen-takes-Rook! (See Diagram E.)

Sherwin

Fischer

Diagram E
. . . after Queen-takes-Rook!

46

yes
(White's Rook is protected by the Bishop.)

47

Is Black mated in this position?

☐ yes
☐ no

If not, draw the usual arrow to show the defense.

better in mind: I interposed my Queen! (See Diagram B.)

Sherwin

Fischer

Diagram B
the Queen has interposed!

Here Black was faced with the threat of Rook-takes-Rook-mate! Taking my queen wouldn't have helped him because I could then have played Rook-takes-Rook, "discovering" a check with my Bishop. (See Diagram C below.)

Sherwin

Fischer

Diagram C (variation)
Check by the Bishop!

47

yes
(Black is mated. White sacrificed his Queen to achieve this mate. Note Black's Bishop next to White's King.)

48

Here is a position from one of my games. Draw an arrow showing how Black can mate:

SUMMARY

Attacks on the Enemy Pawn Cover

With the conclusion of this chapter, you have at your disposal several weapons and techniques necessary to force mate. Here is an extremely difficult combination from my game with James Sherwin in the 1957 United States Championship. The main theme is similar to one you've seen in this book.

Here is the critical position:

Sherwin

Diagram A

Fischer (to move)

I (White) played Rook-takes-Pawn! If Black had then played Rook-takes-Rook, he would have been mated (do you see how?). Sherwin actually played his Rook to my back rank, giving check. I could have interposed with my Rook, giving check with my Bishop ("discovered check!") while doing so, but I had something

48

NOTE: This position is from my game with Letelier (White) in the Leipzig team tournament, 1960. Letelier resigned rather than permit the Bishop to mate.

49

PINS

Observe the differences in each of the following three pairs:

A1. In this position, Black's Queen can capture the attacker.

A2. But here, Black's Queen cannot capture the attacker. The Queen is "pinned" by White's Bishop (i.e., capturing would expose the Black King to capture).

(continued)

239

yes

(Black plays Pawn-takes-Knight, White checks by moving his Rook three squares to the right, Queen-takes-Rook, the other Rook takes the Queen, checkmate.)

NOW TURN THE PAGE AND CONTINUE

49 (continued)

B1. Black's Knight can interpose to defend against the White Rook's check.

B2. The Black Knight <u>cannot</u> interpose (it's pinned by White Queen).

C1. White's Queen can check—and mate.

C2. The White Queen <u>cannot</u> check (it's pinned by Black Rook).

NOW TURN THE PAGE AND CONTINUE WITH FRAME 50

238

(When the Black King moves, the Queen mates on square K. This position is from my 1957 game with Arthur Feuerstein in New York. He avoided this position only at the cost of giving up material, and lost soon anyway.)

239

Can White mate?

☐ yes

☐ no

If so, draw an arrow to show his first move.

49

NO ANSWER REQUIRED

50

Black is mated. A fantastic position! Black's Queen, Bishop and Knight are all "pinned" and thus unable to come to the defense of the Black King.

What White piece prevents Black's Queen from capturing the checking Rook? _______________

What White piece prevents the Black Bishop from interposing? _______________

What White piece prevents Black's Knight from interposing? _______________

237

no
(The Queen sacrifice does not work. At the end, the Black Bishop is waiting to capture White's Rook.)

238

White has forced Black to make a Pawn weakness in front of his King. Draw an arrow showing White's first move in a mating combination:

50

Queen

Rook (next to White King)

Bishop

51

White has several checks, but only one mate.

Which move mates?

- ☐ Bishop-takes-Queen
- ☐ Queen-takes-Queen
- ☐ Queen-takes-Pawn
- ☐ Knight checks

236

yes

(After Black plays King-takes-Rook, White delivers mate with the remaining Rook. White's Queen cannot mate because it is needed to cover the two potential fleeing squares at X and Y.)

237

Can White mate?

☐ yes
☐ no

If so, draw an arrow to show his first move.

51

Knight checks
(Black Queen is pinned by Bishop; Black Pawn is pinned by Queen. Whenever a piece is pinned to the King, it loses most of its powers. Always examine pins carefully because they are the seeds of many combinations.)

52

Observe all pieces carefully!

a. Is Queen checks (as shown) mate?
 ☐ yes
 ☐ no
b. Is Rook-checks mate?
 ☐ yes
 ☐ no

235

yes

(The Knight check drives the King into the corner. Then Rook-takes-Pawn-check; King-takes-Rook; Rook over mates.)

236

Can White mate?

☐ yes

☐ no

If so, draw an arrow to show his first move.

52

a. yes
(Black's Queen is pinned and cannot interpose.)

b. no
(Black's Bishop can capture!)

53

Why can't White's Queen mate as shown?

____

234

yes

(On King-takes-Queen, Rook over mates.)

235

Can White mate?

☐ yes

☐ no

If so, draw an arrow to show his first move.

53

White's Queen is pinned by the Black Rook! Otherwise it could mate, since Black's Queen and Knight are both pinned.

54

Let's review the rule of Pawn promotion. When your Pawn advances all the way to the other end of the board, it becomes a Queen, Rook, Bishop or Knight, according to your choice.

Here White's Pawn can advance and mate Black.

To do so, it must become a:

- ☐ Bishop
- ☐ Knight
- ☐ Queen
- ☐ Rook

233

Knight checks

Rook-takes-Pawn-check
(Then White's third move is to move his other Rook over to the right, giving mate.)

234

You have now learned several ways to push home mates when the enemy King is hemmed in on the corner. In each of the following positions, decide whether any one of those themes is available to White.

Can White mate?

☐ yes

☐ no

If so, draw an arrow to show his first move.

54

Queen
(Promotion to a Rook would not work because the Black King could escape to a flight square. Usually it is best to promote a Pawn to a Queen, since the Queen is the strongest piece. On rare occasions, however, promoting to a weaker piece [e.g., Knight] is a better play.)

55

Believe it or not, White can mate in this position:

The correct White move is:

- ☐ Pawn advances straight ahead and becomes a Knight
- ☐ Pawn advances straight ahead and becomes a Queen
- ☐ Pawn takes Bishop and becomes a Queen
- ☐ Pawn takes Bishop and becomes a Bishop

232

Queen-takes-Rook-check
(After King-takes-Queen, Rook down mates. Note that here the Knight check fails because Black can reply with Rook-takes-Knight-check.)

233

This position looks harmless, but White can mate in three moves by first driving the King into the corner, and then mating with one of the themes you have learned.

What is White's first move? ______________

What is the second White move? ______________

55

Pawn advances straight ahead and becomes a Knight
(Black is mated, as shown. Had White made a Queen instead, Black would have queened his Pawn too—with check.)

56

In this position, a White Pawn can promote and mate:

To mate, the Pawn should:

- ☐ advance straight ahead
- ☐ take the Knight

What must it become if it is to mate? ______________

231

Knight checks
(After Black plays Pawn-takes-Knight, White mates with his Rook. The important feature is that White can reach the vertical file leading to Black's King with one of his heavy pieces—Queen or, as here, Rook—to give mate.)

232

What is White's key first move in this position?

- ☐ Knight checks
- ☐ Queen-takes-Pawn-check
- ☐ Queen-takes-Rook-check

56

advance straight ahead

Queen <u>or</u> Rook

57

Here is a review of some of the material you've learned.

Observe this position:

Can White's Queen mate?

☐ yes

☐ no

Can White's Knight mate?

☐ yes

☐ no

230

Queen-takes-Pawn-check
(Then on Rook-takes-Queen, Rook down mates.)

231

What is White's key first move in this position?

- ☐ Knight checks
- ☐ Queen-takes-Pawn-check
- ☐ Queen-takes-Rook-check

57

no
(Neither of the Queen checks will be mate.)

yes
(Black Pawn is pinned by White Rook.)

58

Here is a complex position. Observe all pieces carefully.

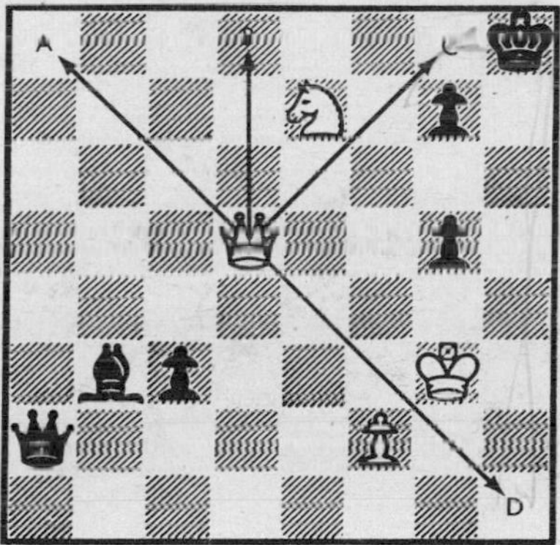

The Queen has several checks. The only one that mates is at square:

☐ A
☐ B
☐ C
☐ D

229

NO ANSWER REQUIRED

230

The next three positions look somewhat similar, but each allows for a different type of mating combination by White.

What is White's key first move in this position?

- ☐ Knight checks
- ☐ Queen-takes-Pawn-check
- ☐ Queen-takes-Rook-check

58

D

59

Observe the board carefully.

White's Queen and Knight have checks.

Draw an arrow showing the mating White move:

229 (continued)

C. The White Queen delivers the mate.

NOW TURN THE PAGE AND CONTINUE WITH FRAME 230

59

(This position is a smothered mate—Black's own pieces prevent him from fleeing from check.)

60

Here White's Pawn, Queen and Rook have checks.

Draw an arrow to show the one mating move:

228

(Then the other Rook moves one square to the left to mate.)

229

A. Here White follows a slightly different theme in bringing about mate.

B. The key first move is a check by White's Knight. Since Black's King cannot move, the Black Pawn must capture.

(continued)

60

61

White's Pawn and Queen can check, but only one of them mates.

Which one?

☐ Pawn

☐ Queen

227

(After Rook-takes-Pawn-check, King-takes-Rook, the Queen moves four squares to the right to give mate.)

228

Draw an arrow to show the first move in the White mating combination:

61

Pawn
(Black's Rook is pinned, but would be free to interpose if the White Queen checked.)

62

In choosing the check in this position, you must be careful not to allow the Black King any flight squares.

Which White move (as shown) mates?

- ☐ move by White Queen
- ☐ move by White Rook

226

(. . . and mate on the next move.)

227

Draw an arrow to show the first move in the White mating combination:

62

move by White Rook

(The Queen check would allow Black two fleeing squares, as shown above.)

63

Here's a fancy one.

When the White Rook moves, the White Bishop will be checking. (This is called a "discovered check.") The Rook has an opportunity to move to a square that cuts off the Black King's flight squares.

Draw an arrow to show the mate:

225

(Queen-takes-Pawn-check; Rook-takes-Queen; Rook down checks; Rook next to King interposes; Bishop checks; and mate next move by Rook-takes-Rook.)

226

Draw an arrow to show the first move in the White mating combination:

63

64

In this and the following frame, you will have to select the mates from among a number of tempting checks. I've made the positions a little tricky, so be careful!

In the first position there are four checks, but only one mate. Be accurate! Black threatens mate, too.

Draw the usual arrow to show White's mating move:

224

no

(Not if Black replies with Queen-takes-Queen! On King-takes-Queen, White would mate.)

225

In some of the following positions, White utilizes the theme you have just learned in order to mate. In others, he mates in a different way.

Draw an arrow to show the first move in the White mating combination:

64

65

Here is the second position. Again, show the mate by an arrow.

223

no!
(White does not mate. After White plays Queen-takes-Pawn-check, Black's King takes Queen and the Rook moves over to the left, giving check, Black can interpose with his Rook.)

224

Does White have a mating combination beginning with Queen-takes-Pawn (as shown)?

☐ yes
☐ no

65

(The Black Rook, pinned by one of White's Bishops, stands by powerless while the other White Bishop protects the Queen from capture by Black's King. The Queen cuts off Black's one flight square—Black could flee if White moved his Queen straight down to the last rank.)

66

In this next series of frames you will be shown various positions. In some, White can mate Black in one move; in others, White has many checks, but <u>no</u> mates. You will have to decide whether White can mate, and if so, how.

In this position:

- ☐ White can mate in one move
- ☐ White cannot mate

If there is a mate, draw an arrow to show White's mating move.

222

no

(The Black King will have a flight square.)

223

Does White have a mating combination beginning with Queen-takes-Pawn (as shown)?

☐ yes
☐ no

66

White can mate in one move

67

In this position:

- ☐ White can mate in one move
- ☐ White cannot mate

If there is a mate, draw an arrow to show White's mating move.

221

yes
(White mates. Here the White Knight keeps the Black King from fleeing.)

222

Does White have a mating combination beginning with Queen-takes-Pawn-check (as shown)?

☐ yes
☐ no

67

White can mate in one move

68

In this position:

- ☐ White can mate in one move
- ☐ White cannot mate

If White can mate, draw an arrow to show his mating move.

220

yes
(White mates: Queen-takes-Pawn-check; King-takes-Queen; Rook over to the right; checkmate.)

221

Does White have a mating combination beginning with Queen-takes-Pawn (as shown)?

☐ yes
☐ no

68

White cannot mate

69

Here's a position from a game I played:

Can White mate in one move?

☒ yes

☐ no

If "yes," draw an arrow to show White's mating move.

219

NO ANSWER REQUIRED

220

Decide whether the type of sacrifice shown in the previous frame works in each of the five positions that follow.

Does White have a mating combination beginning with Queen-takes-Pawn-check (as shown)?

☐ yes

☐ no

69

no
(The Knight check is met by the Queen's capture of the Knight! This position is from my game with Otteson [White] in 1957.)

70

In this position:

- ☐ White can mate in one move
- ☐ White cannot mate

If there is a mate, draw an arrow to show the mating move.

219 (continued)

C. The Black King has been forced to capture. And now White's Queen mates. Notice that the King is hemmed in. The position is almost like a back-rank mate.

NOW TURN THE PAGE AND CONTINUE WITH FRAME 220

70

White can mate in one move

(White mates on square B. He cannot mate on square A because the Black Queen defends that square.)

71

In this position:

- ☐ White can mate in one move
- ☐ White cannot mate

If there is a mate, draw an arrow to show the mating move.

218

(After Queen-takes-Pawn-check, Rook takes Queen, Rook checks, Rook interposes, the circled White Rook [by now down on Black's back rank] captures the Black Rook, giving checkmate. In the final position, the Rook giving mate is supported by the other White Rook.)

219

A. Here the Queen sacrifice doesn't work, but . . .

B. . . . the Rook sacrifice does!

(continued)

71

White cannot mate
(In fact, any White piece that dares to check will be promptly captured.)

72

In this position:

- ☐ White can mate in one move
- ☐ White cannot mate

If White can mate, draw an arrow to show his mating move.

217

(Here, after Queen-takes-Pawn-check, Rook takes Queen, Rook checks, Rook interposes [other interpositions are useless], and the Bishop next to the King moves up and mates on square X.)

218

Circle the White piece that administers mate, assuming Black captures the Queen:

72

White can mate in one move

(One of White's Rooks keeps the Black King imprisoned, while the other delivers the mate!)

73

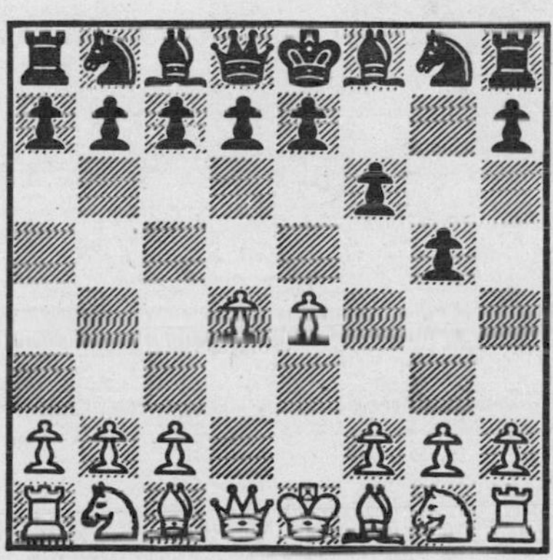

Can White mate in one move?

☐ yes

☐ no

If "yes," draw an arrow to show White's mating move.

216

(This one is tricky—after Queen-takes-Pawn-check, Rook takes Queen, Rook interposes and White pushes up his Pawn, checkmate.)

217

Circle the White piece that administers mate:

73

yes

(Black foolishly weakened his King's defenses. This game took three moves!!)

74

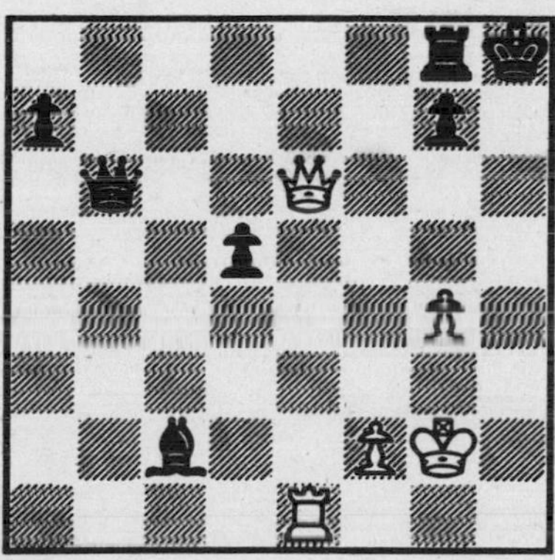

In this position:

- ☐ White can mate in one move
- ☐ White cannot mate

If White can mate in one move, draw an arrow to show his mating move.

215

(After Queen-takes-Pawn-check followed by Rook-takes-Queen, Rook [in center] checks, Rook interposes and Bishop gives mate.)

216

Circle the White piece that administers mate:

74

White cannot mate

75

This is a position from one of my games:

Can Black mate in one move?

☐ yes

☐ no

If "yes," indicate his mating move with an arrow.

214

(After Queen-takes-Pawn-check, Rook-takes-Queen, Rook down leads to mate.)

215

Circle the White piece that administers mate:

75

yes

76

Can White mate in one move?

☐ yes

☐ no

If "yes," draw an arrow to indicate the mating move.

213

the Bishop

214

You have seen how, in certain positions, the key move Queen-takes-Pawn-check draws a defender from the back rank and leads to mate. In this series of frames, you will be asked to work out the whole combination and to circle the White piece that delivers the checkmate.

Assume, here, that Black captures the Queen.

76

no
(Observe both Black Bishops.)

77

In the position above:

- ☐ White can mate in one move
- ☐ White cannot mate

If there is a mate, draw an arrow to show the move.

212

NO ANSWER REQUIRED

213

One other variation:

1. White's Queen takes Pawn, giving check (Black's Rook must capture).
2. White's Rook checks, etc.

What White piece actually delivers the mate?

____

77

White can mate in one move

(The Black Queen is pinned.)

78

Can White mate in one move?

☐ yes

☐ no

If "yes," show the mating move with an arrow.

212 (continued)

C. Now look at the position. It's two against one and a back-rank mate. White can mate with either Rook.

NOW TURN THE PAGE AND CONTINUE WITH FRAME 213

78

yes

(Pawn mates by becoming a Queen or a Rook. Note that the White Bishop, which is itself pinned, pins one of the Black Rooks.)

79

Can White mate in one move?

☐ yes

☐ no

If "yes," draw an arrow to show the mating move.

211

by moving his King away
(If, instead, he plays Queen-takes-Queen, White would mate with this line of play: White Rook checks; Rook-takes-Rook; Rook-takes-Rook-checkmate.)

212

A. Here the White Queen has taken the Pawn, with check, and Black's Rook captures.

B. White's Rook checks and Black's Rook must interpose.

(continued)

79

yes

(Again, the pin wins.)

THIS IS THE END OF CHAPTER 1

NOW TURN THE PAGE AND GO ON TO CHAPTER 2

210

yes
(White mates. After Black plays Rook-takes-Queen, White checks with his Rook on the back rank; Black interposes with his Rook; and then White checks with his Bishop—driving the Black King into the corner and making possible Rook-takes-Rook-mate.)

211

You must have figured one of these positions would not be a mate. So on this one, I'll ask you something else.

After the Queen check, how can Black save himself?

☐ by moving his King away
☐ by playing Queen-takes-Queen

Chapter 2

THE BACK-RANK MATES

This chapter presents the basic elements of the most common of all mating combinations: the back-rank mates (i.e., mates accomplished on the row of squares at the near or far side of the board). These mates often involve several moves for both sides, some of which are fairly simple and some not so simple.

TURN THE PAGE AND CONTINUE WITH FRAME 80

209

yes

210

Does the sacrifice work here?

- ☐ yes
- ☐ no

80

USEFUL VERSUS USELESS INTERPOSITION

A. Black is in check. He can interpose his Bishop, as shown, but the White Rook will simply capture it and mate. In this case, the interposition is useless.

B. But here when the Black Bishop interposes it will be protected by the Black King. This interposition is useful—White cannot mate.

C. Here Black's Rook can make a useful interposition; it will be protected by the other Black Rook.

D. In this position, either the Black Knight or the Black Bishop can make a useful interposition since one will protect the other.

NOW TURN THE PAGE AND CONTINUE WITH FRAME 81

208

NO ANSWER REQUIRED

209

Check the following position to see if all of the elements for the mating combination are present:

Does the Queen check (as shown) lead to mate?

☐ yes

☐ no

80

NO ANSWER REQUIRED

81

Observe the position and then decide whether Black has a useful interposition against the check.

Does Black have a useful interposition?

☐ yes
☐ no

208 (continued)

C. Black's Rook has captured, allowing White's Rook to check.

D. White's Rook has checked; Black has a simple defense: Rook interposes. Black must resist the impulse to play Rook-takes-Rook first—that move would lose the game for him.

E. The White Bishop checks, driving the King into the corner. Everything has gone as planned . . .

F. . . . but wait a minute! What is White going to do now? Nothing. Black's back rank is sound. White cannot mate and has lost his Queen. But if Black had traded Rooks, White would now be able to play Rook-takes-Rook mate.

81

yes
(Black has a useful interposition, with either the Rook or the Bishop.)

82

Does Black have a useful interposition?

☐ yes
☐ no

207

King!
(Capture by the Black Rook loses.)

208

See how the sacrifice fails miserably in this position:

A. Here goes the White Queen . . .

B. The White Queen has captured the Pawn, with check.

(continued)

82

yes
(Black has a useful interposition, with the Knight.)

83

Does Black have a useful interposition?

- ☐ yes
- ☐ no

206

NO ANSWER REQUIRED

207

You must be certain all of the elements in the combination are present. Otherwise, you'll simply throw away your Queen.

Here is a position where the White Queen has sacrificed (as shown). It looks as if the sacrifice will work, but it doesn't. Black saves himself by capturing the Queen with his ______________.

83

no
(Black's interpositions are useless; therefore, White mates.)

84

Does Black have a useful interposition?

☐ yes
☐ no

206 (continued)

C. White's Rook checks, but this time Black's Rook can interpose.

D. But now the White Bishop can drive away Black's King. You've seen this part of the combination before. White mates.

NOW TURN THE PAGE AND CONTINUE WITH FRAME 207

84

yes

85

Draw an arrow to show the useful interposition for Black in this position:

205

NOTE: Queen-takes-Pawn-check leads to mate. This position is from my 1959 game with the Swiss Master, Bhend. I was White but it was actually my move—not Black's! Moving the Rook three squares horizontally—between the Black Queen and Rook—stops both threats.

206

In this position, White combines the theme of attack against the Pawn near the King with one of the displacing themes.

A. White starts by giving up his Queen: Queen-takes-Pawn-check.

B. The White Queen has made its check, and Black's Rook will capture (note that White's Knight prevents Black's King from capturing).

(continued)

85

(The Bishop move is the only useful interposition. The Black Queen is pinned and the Black Rook, if it interposes, will not bc protected by the pinned Queen.)

86

Draw an arrow to show the useful interposition here:

204

White's Rook will not be able to check
(It is pinned.)

205

From a game of mine.

If you were Black what would you play here? Think! Black has two threats—one is obvious, but the other . . .

Draw an arrow showing Black's best move.

86

87

What is Black's defense against checkmate in this position? ________________

203

Black's Knight captures the Queen
(Otherwise, Black will be mated.)

204

A White move of Queen-takes-Pawn-check does not lead to mate because ______________

87

Black's Knight takes Queen! (The only saving move.)

88

Observe the combination in the diagrams below:

A. White's Queen and two Rooks are lined up on the "open" file leading down to Black's back rank.

B. White's Queen has checked, and the Black Rook must capture it.

(continued)

202

Black's Bishop will be able to interpose
(After Black plays Queen-takes-Queen, White Rook checks and Black saves himself as above.)

203

A White move of Queen-takes-Pawn-check does not lead to mate because ________________.

88 (continued)

C. White now plays Rook-takes-Rook, thus giving check.

D. Black must recapture (Queen takes Rook).

E. And now the other White Rook can mate.

NOW TURN THE PAGE AND CONTINUE WITH FRAME 89

201

yes
(The sacrifice works—White mates.)

202

Here are some positions where the theme you have learned does not apply. In each case, you will be asked to explain why this is so.

A White move of Queen-takes-Pawn-check does not lead to mate because ________________

89

DETERMINING AMOUNT OF POWER NEEDED TO MATE

Study the following positions:

A. This first position is an example of two against two: the two White Rooks are ready to give check on the same Black back-rank square; the Black Rook and Black Bishop are ready to capture. White cannot mate.

B. Here again we have two against two: two White Rooks attacking the same back-rank square; two pieces, the Knight and the King, act as defenders. There is no mate for White.

(continued)

200

no
(White does not mate since Black's King has a flight square. Black should play Rook-takes-Queen and then flee with his King when White checks with his Rook.)

201

Does the White move of Queen-takes-Pawn-check (as shown) lead to mate?

☐ yes
☐ no

89 (continued)

C. In this position, White has more power (three against two) and can mate. Rook checks; Knight takes Rook; Rook takes Knight, mate. In the final position, the second White Rook is supported by the Bishop. Without the Bishop, Black could play King-takes-Rook.

D. Two against one: the White Queen and Rook attack the same back-rank square; only a Rook defends. White mates.

(continued)

199

yes
(A mate for White! If Black plays Queen-takes-Queen, then the White Rook mates.)

200

Does the White move of Queen-takes-Pawn-check (as shown) lead to mate?

☐ yes
☐ no

89 (continued)

E. Also two against one. Note that the Black Rook does not count because it will be captured on the first check. White mates.

F. Here it's two against two, with no White mate. A third White piece (the Bishop) attacks the same back-rank square, but will not give check.

G. The White Queen is pinned and unable to move forward, but it can still play a supportive role. The White Rook move is checkmate.

NOW TURN THE PAGE AND CONTINUE WITH FRAME 90

198

yes
(Here the Bishop is present. When Black plays Rook-takes-Queen, the White Rook will mate.)

199

Does the White move of Queen-takes-Pawn-check (as shown) lead to mate?

☐ yes
☐ no

89

NO ANSWER REQUIRED

90

The next series of frames will show various positions You will be asked to determine whether White has enough power to mate on Black's back rank. You must observe all of the pieces on the board.

Does White have enough power to mate on Black's back rank?

☐ yes
☐ no

197

no
(Black's King or Rook can safely take the Queen. An important element of the theme—the White Bishop—is missing.)

198

Does Queen-takes-Pawn-check lead to mate here?

☐ yes
☐ no

90

yes
(White has the power to mate—four against three. The last check will be given by Rook <u>supported by Bishop</u>.)

91

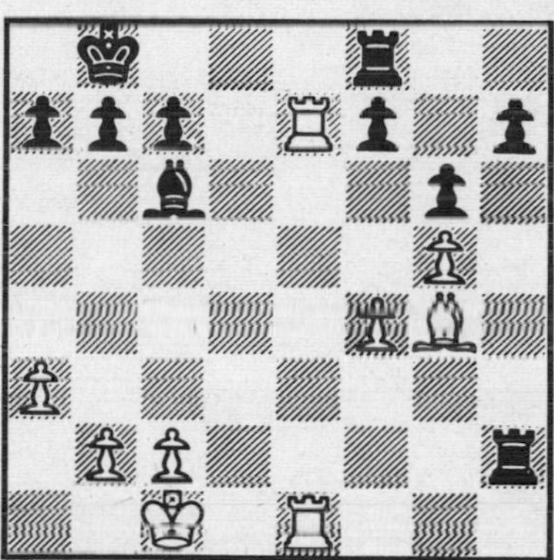

Does White have enough power to mate on Black's back rank?

☐ yes
☐ no

196

NO ANSWER REQUIRED

197

In the next four positions, you will have to determine whether a sacrifice similar to the one that you've just seen will lead to mate.

Does the White move of Queen-takes-Pawn-check (as shown) lead to mate?

☐ yes
☐ no

91

no
(There is no mate here—two against two: Black Bishop and Rook against two Rooks.)

92

Does White have enough power to mate on Black's back rank?

☐ yes
☐ no

196

Let's look at this position again:

A. White's Queen has captured the Pawn with check. Black decides to move his King.

B. Now White can play Queen-takes-Rook-mate.

NOW TURN THE PAGE AND CONTINUE WITH FRAME 197

92

yes
(White has the power: White Queen and two Rooks against only two defenders.)

93

Does White have enough power to mate on Black's back rank?

☐ yes
☐ no

195

Observe how mate is accomplished in the diagrams below:

A. In this position, White has a simple mate in two moves but he must find the key first move. All other moves lose the game for him.

B. White's key first move: Queen-captures-Pawn-check, sacrificing his Queen.

C. Black's Rook captures the Queen. (Note that the Black King could not capture because of White's Bishop.)

D. The check by White's Rook does it! Black's Rook cannot interpose (it's pinned).

NOW TURN THE PAGE AND CONTINUE WITH FRAME 196

93

no
(One against one. White cannot mate. The White Bishop and Knight attack the back-rank square, but do not check when they land on it—so, as far as the back-rank mating combination is concerned, they don't really count.)

94

Does White have enough power to mate on Black's back rank?

☐ yes
☐ no

Chapter 5

ATTACKS ON THE ENEMY PAWN COVER

Sometimes your opponent's King appears completely secure with his own pieces surrounding him on all sides, when in fact he can easily be mated by a sacrifice that breaks up his defense. All of the themes in this chapter involve sacrifices that demolish the Pawn structure in front of the enemy King.

TURN THE PAGE AND CONTINUE WITH FRAME 195

94

yes
(It's two against one. The White Rook and the White Pawn attack the square. The Pawn will promote to a Queen or Rook, giving mate.)

95

In the following positions, White threatens the Black back rank, but <u>cannot</u> mate. You must decide why Black escapes the mate: Has he enough power to defend against White's attack? Or, will he have a flight square or a useful interposition?

Why does White's threat against Black's back rank <u>not</u> lead to mate?

- ☐ White does not have enough power to mate.
- ☐ The Black King will have a flight square.
- ☐ Black has a useful interposition.

SUMMARY
Displacing Defenders

Here is an example of mating by driving the King into the corner. From my game with Herbert Seidman (White) in the 1957 United States Championship:

White would like to capture my Bishop and be ahead in material by two Pawns. Let's see what would happen. Suppose White plays Rook-takes-Bishop. I then play Rook-takes-Rook and White recaptures with his Queen, giving this position:

Now I (Black) can play Queen-takes-Pawn-check, driving the King into the corner. Then it's a simple mate after the Queen checks on White's back rank.

THIS IS THE END OF CHAPTER 4
NOW TURN THE PAGE AND GO ON TO CHAPTER 5

95

The Black King will have a flight square.
(The White Queen will no longer guard it.)

96

Why does White's threat against Black's back rank not lead to mate?

- ☐ White does not have enough power to mate.
- ☐ The Black King will have a flight square.
- ☐ Black has a useful interposition.

194

(The back-rank defenders are reduced from two to one after the King is forced to move.)

NOW TURN THE PAGE AND CONTINUE

96

Black has a useful interposition.
(The Bishop interposes. Black could also play Rook-takes-Rook, Pawn-takes-Rook becoming a Queen with check, and then interpose; but this doesn't make much sense because White would gain a new Queen.)

97

Why does White's threat against Black's back rank <u>not</u> lead to mate?

- ☐ White does not have enough power to mate.
- ☐ The Black King will have a flight square.
- ☐ Black has a useful interposition.

193

(First the King is driven into the corner; then White has power to mate on the back rank.)

194

Draw an arrow to show the first move for White in his mating combination:

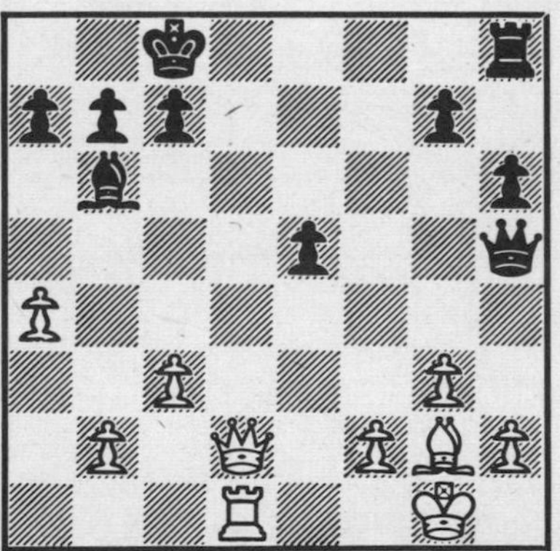

97

White does not have enough power to mate.
(Black Queen and Bishop guard the square on the back rank.)

98

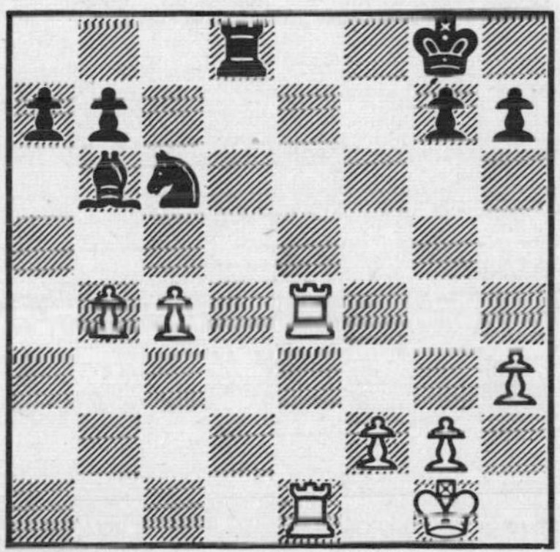

Why does White's threat against Black's back rank not lead to mate?

- ☐ White does not have enough power to mate.
- ☐ The Black King will have a flight square.
- ☐ Black has a useful interposition.

192

(After taking the Pawn, the White Bishop is safe from capture by either the Black King or Rook. Black's King must therefore move into the corner. Then Rook-takes-Rook is mate.)

193

Draw an arrow to show the first move for White in his mating combination:

98

The Black King will have a flight square.

99

In this position, focus your attention on the White and Black Queens:

Now explain in your own words why White cannot mate.

191

(The Black Bishop captures the Rook; then the remaining White Rook will mate.)

192

Draw an arrow to show the first move for White in his mating combination:

99

The White Queen is pinned.
(If the White Rook checks, Black's Rook simply captures, and the White Queen cannot recapture the Rook.)

100

Here is a position from one of my games (Fischer vs. Bisguier, New York, 1957), where I (White) had to decide whether or not I should capture Bisguier's (Black) Queen with my Rook.

Would you capture Black's Queen?

☐ yes

☐ no

Explain your answer. ________________

190

(. . . followed by Rook check on the back rank.)

191

Draw an arrow to show the first move for White in his mating combination:

100

no
Black would recapture with his Rook, giving check and forcing mate. White then has only useless interpositions.

(Bisguier is a former U.S. Champion. I made a different move—Rook four squares to the left—and won the game.)

101

To which square should the White Queen move to begin its mating combination?

- ☐ A
- ☐ B
- ☐ C

189

(If the Pawn captures the Knight, a safe White Queen check will force the Black King into the corner, and then Rook-takes-Rook will be mate.

If the King moves into the corner immediately, Rook-takes-Rook is mate.)

190

Draw an arrow to show the first move for White in his mating combination:

101

B
(Of course—the other two checks allow Black to capture White's Queen.)

102

To which square should White move in this position?

- ☐ A
- ☐ B
- ☐ C

188

(And White mates with his Rook on the next move.)

189

Draw an arrow to show the first move for White in his mating combination:

102

C
(The other moves would allow Black to escape mate.)

103

Draw an arrow showing the first move of White's mating combination:

187

(White forces the Black King into the corner, thereby giving himself enough power to mate.)

188

Draw an arrow to show the first move for White in his mating combination:

103

(After Black captures White's Rook, White will recapture with the Pawn making a Queen or Rook.)

104

Should White check with the Rook or the Queen?

☐ with the Rook

☐ with the Queen

186

(The Bishop check will not work because Black's Knight can interpose at square X, thereby stopping all mates.)

187

Draw an arrow to show the first move for White in his mating combination:

104

with the Queen
(The Queen checkmates. If White's Rook checks, the Black Knight can interpose on the square protected by Black's Queen; there is no mate then because the Black Bishop prevents the White Queen from checking.)

105

Assume that White elects to check in this position; then decide whether he will be able to force mate.

Does White have a mating combination beginning with a back-rank check?

☐ yes ☐ no

If "no," why?

☐ not enough power
☐ flight square for Black King
☐ useful interposition

185

yes
(The White Queen will be able to drive the Black King into the corner if Black captures the Knight. The White Rook will be the mating piece.)

186

REVIEW

White can mate in all of the positions shown in this next series of frames. Sometimes he does so in one move, sometimes by a back-rank combination, sometimes by a move that displaces the enemy King or an enemy piece.

Draw an arrow to show the correct move for White in his mating combination:

105

yes
(White mates. Interposition is useless.)

106

Does White have a mating combination beginning with a back-rank check?

☐ yes
☐ no

If "no," why?

☐ not enough power
☐ flight squares for Black King
☐ useful interposition

184

no!

(Black plays Pawn-takes-Knight; then after White's Rook checks, Black's Rook interposes, protected by a Pawn. If the Knight checks on the other square, the same kind of situation results.)

185

Does the White Knight check work here?

☐ yes
☐ no

106

yes
(White mates. Rook and Queen give him enough power.)

107

Does White have a mating combination beginning with a back-rank check?

☐ yes
☐ no

If "no," why?

☐ not enough power
☐ flight square for Black King
☐ useful interposition

183

yes

yes
(In either case, Black's Pawn must capture. White's Queen can then drive the Black King into the corner.)

184

Here White attempts to drive away the Black King, beginning with Knight checks. Decide whether the move succeeds.

Does the White Knight's check (as shown) lead to mate?

- ☐ yes
- ☐ no

107

no

flight square for Black King

NOTE: Here's why it doesn't work. After White "queens" his Pawn—thereby giving check—Black captures the new Queen with his Rook. White then captures the Black Rook with his Rook, giving this position:

108

Does White have a mating combination beginning with a back-rank check?

☐ yes

☐ no

If "no," why?

☐ not enough power

☐ flight square for Black King

☐ useful interposition

182

Knight captures
(If Pawn captures, the White Rook check on the newly opened line will drive the King into the corner [see diagram], and the other Rook will mate.
If the King moves, then Rook captures Bishop, giving mate.)

183

Does a check by White's Knight at square A lead to mate?

☐ yes
☐ no

Does a check by White's Knight at square B lead to mate?

☐ yes
☐ no

108

no

not enough power
(An example of two against two: Black's Bishop and Knight guard the checking square against the two attacking White Rooks.)

109

Does White have a mating combination beginning with a back-rank check?

☐ yes
☐ no

If "no," why?

☐ not enough power
☐ flight squares for Black King
☐ useful interposition

181

NO ANSWER REQUIRED

182

White's Knight has checked. Black can save himself by playing:

- ☐ King moves
- ☐ Pawn captures
- ☐ Knight captures

109

no

useful interposition (Bishop)

110

Does White have a mating combination beginning with a back-rank check?

☐ yes
☐ no

If "no," why?

☐ not enough power
☐ flight squares for Black King
☐ useful interposition

181 (continued)

C. If Black allows his King to be driven into the corner, his Queen will be left unprotected. His only other move is Pawn-captures-Knight.

D. And now the idea becomes clear! We have here an example of the driving away theme. The White Rook checks (and after Black's King moves, White's Queen will mate).

NOW TURN THE PAGE AND CONTINUE WITH FRAME 182

110

yes
(White mates. The second Rook delivers mate, supported by the Knight.)

111

In this next series of frames, you will have to consider several positions. In some, White has a back-rank combination. In others, he has a one-move mate of a different type. In a few, he has no mate at all. Most of these positions are difficult, posing many possibilities. Observe all of the pieces on the board for Black defenses. If the back-rank check does not lead to mate, look for other checks that might do so.

In this position, White:

- ☐ can mate
- ☐ cannot mate

If there is a mate, draw an arrow to show White's key first move.

180

(Here White can reach the same mating position in two ways: (1) Bishop-takes-Pawn-check; King one square to the left; Queen to the back rank, check; Rook-takes-Queen, Rook-takes-Rook-mate. (2) Queen to back rank, check; Rook-takes-Queen; Bishop-takes-Pawn-check; King one square to the left; Rook-takes-Rook-mate. Incidentally, the Bishop check at square X permits Black to interpose with his Pawn at square Y.)

181

One more subtlety of the displacing themes.

A. Observe this position. It looks harmless enough. But, White can force mate.

B. First move in the combination: Knight checks as shown.

(continued)

111

can mate

(White makes a Queen with his Pawn, giving check. If Black captures the Queen with his Rook, White will recapture with the White Rook, giving mate.)

112

In this position:

☐ White can mate

☐ White cannot mate

If there is a mate, show it (that is, the key first move).

179

(The White Queen can't drive away the Black King because the Black Queen guards the important square.)

180

Unless you look closely at this one, you won't see all of White's attempts and you'll miss the winning move.

Draw an arrow to show the move for White that leads to mate:

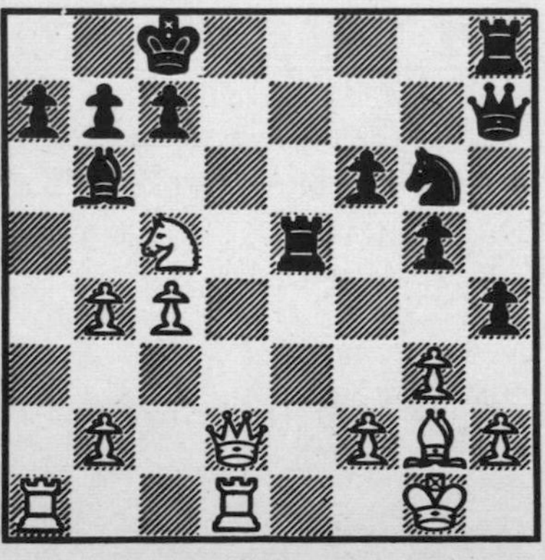

12

Vhite can mate
Black has only useless
nterpositions with his
Bishop and Queen.)

13

In this position:

☐ White can mate

☐ White cannot mate

If there is a mate, show it.

.78

(Black must move his King into the corner; then White mates by playing Queen-takes-Queen.)

.79

)raw an arrow to show the winning move for White:

113

White cannot mate
(If the White Queen checks on Black's back rank, the Bishop will interpose. Or, if the Queen checks four squares straight ahead, Black can flee.)

114

In this position:

☐ White can mate

☐ White can't mate

If there is a mate, show it.

177

(Queen-check would lose to Bishop-takes-Queen.)

178

Draw an arrow to show the correct displacing move:

14

White can mate

15

In this position:

- ☐ White can mate
- ☐ White can't mate

If there is a mate, show it.

176

to square B
(Then White will mate on the back rank. From square A White would not have enough power to mate on the back rank.)

177

Here White could try to displace <u>either</u> the King <u>or</u> another defender. Draw an arrow to show his correct move:

115

White can mate
(All interpositions are useless.)

116

In this position:

- ☐ White can mate
- ☐ White can't mate

If there is a mate, show it.

175

Bishop to square A
(Queen-takes-Queen would be Black's reply to the White Queen check.)

176

How should White's Queen move?

☐ to square A
☐ to square B

116

White can't mate
(White's Rook is pinned so it could not recapture if White checked with the Queen.)

117

In this position:

- ☐ White can mate
- ☐ White can't mate

If there is a mate, show it.

174

a. Black Pawn pushes and interposes.

b. Black Queen takes White Queen.

175

In this position, White has various tries, but only one move works.

What is the correct White move?

☐ Bishop to square A

☐ Queen to square B

117

White can mate

(White has enough power to mate; in moving the Rook, White uncovers his Bishop, thereby freeing it to guard the Black King's only fleeing square.)

118

In this position:

☐ White can mate

☐ White can't mate

If there is a mate, show it.

173

(. . . followed by Queen-takes-Queen-mate.)

174

Let's look at some simple defenses against displacing attempts.

a. How does Black defend against the check by White's Bishop (as shown at square A)? ________________

b. How does Black defend against the White's Queen check, as shown? ________________

118

White can mate

119

In this position:

- ☐ White can mate
- ☐ White can't mate

If there is a mate, show it.

172

(. . . driving the King into the corner to allow Rook-takes-Rook-mate.)

173

Again, draw an arrow to show the correct move for White:

119

White can mate

120

In this position:

- ☐ White can mate
- ☐ White can't mate

If there is a mate, show it.

171

NO ANSWER REQUIRED

172

Draw an arrow to show the correct move for White:

120

White can't mate

121

From one of my recent games:

In this position:

☐ White can mate

☐ White can't mate

If there is a mate, show it!

171 (continued)

D1. Here the White <u>Rook</u> checks.

D2. Black has only one move: the King must move into the corner, allowing White to play Queen-takes-Queen-mate.

E1. Even a lowly Pawn sometimes gets into the act. In this position, White plays Pawn-takes-Pawn-check.

E2. Observe the position now. The checking White Pawn is protected by a Knight. Black's King can only move away and be mated by Queen-takes-Queen.

NOW TURN THE PAGE AND CONTINUE WITH FRAME 172

121

White can mate

(Black is forced to interpose with his Rook; White then plays Queen-takes-Rook and mates. This position could have occurred in my game with the Hungarian Grandmaster Bilek in the 1965 Havana Tournament. My opponent avoided this position.)

122

In this position:

☐ White can mate

☐ White can't mate

If there is a mate, show it.

171 (continued)

B1. White's Rook has checked. Black must interpose his Rook.

B2. And now the White Bishop checks. Black's King must move into the corner (his Rook is pinned and cannot interpose). White will then play Rook-takes-Rook-mate.

C1. The White Queen has checked. Black's Queen must interpose.

C2. White plays Bishop-takes-Pawn-check. What is Black to do? His Queen cannot capture (its pinned), nor can his King. He must move his King into the corner and be mated.

(continued)

122

White can mate

123

In this position:

- ☐ White can mate
- ☐ White can't mate

If there is a mate, show it.

170

no
(Not if Black's <u>Bishop</u> captures. If the Black King moves, White <u>mates</u>.)

171

There are many ways of driving away the Black King. Here are some examples:

A1. White plays Knight check (as shown).

A2. The Black King has been driven into the corner. White can now play Rook-takes-Rook-mate.

(continued)

123

White can mate

(Black's Rook must capture the Queen; then White can recapture with his Rook, giving checkmate.)

124

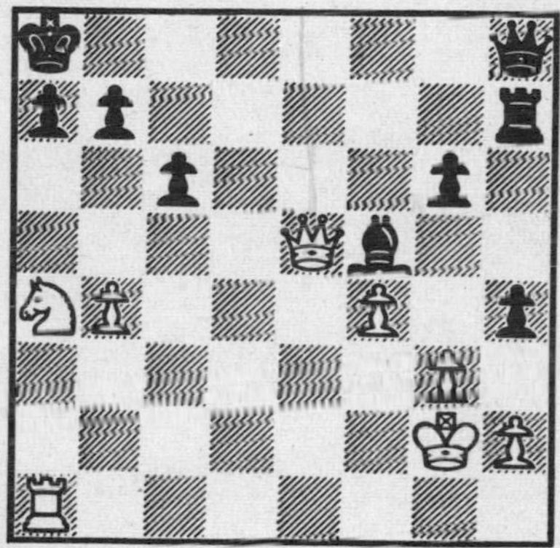

In this position:

- ☐ White can mate
- ☐ White can't mate

If there is a mate, show it.

169

no
(Driving away the King does not work. Black's King is forced away but will have an escape square.)

170

If the White Queen checks (as shown), will White be able to mate?

☐ yes
☐ no

124

White can mate

NOW TURN THE PAGE AND CONTINUE

168

NO ANSWER REQUIRED

169

Can White mate if he first checks (as shown) in this position?

☐ yes
☐ no

SUMMARY
The Back-Rank Mates

In this chapter you were introduced to the elements of the back-rank mate and the three methods of escaping check (and mate): capturing the checking piece, interposing and fleeing.

Here is an example of the back-rank mating theme. The following position came up in my game with Raymond Weinstein (Black) in the 1960 United States Championship (Black to move):

Weinstein

Fischer

I had just captured a Pawn with my Queen. The obvious question was, why couldn't Black capture the Queen with his Rook? Well, if the Rook had captured the Queen, I would have played Rook-check; the Knight would have to take the Rook; and then Rook-takes-Knight would have been mate! The Black Rook could not leave the back rank.

Note also that my Queen was attacking Black's Rook, on the back rank, and Black's Bishop. If Black had attempted to "protect" his Bishop with the attacked Rook, I would simply have played Queen-takes-Bishop! Ray, realizing he was "busted," resigned.

168 (continued)

C. And now White has a simple back-rank mate.

NOW TURN THE PAGE AND CONTINUE WITH FRAME 169

Here is another example from my 1960 United States Championship game with Herbert Seidman (Black):

It's my move and I have to be careful not to think my King is safe. If, for instance, I dare to capture the Black Pawn as shown by arrow 1, Black would mate with his Rook (see arrow 2). Fleeing, as shown by arrow 3, is not possible—the other Rook covers that square!

THIS IS THE END OF CHAPTER 2

NOW TURN THE PAGE AND GO ON TO CHAPTER 3

167

no
(If the White Queen attempts to displace the Black Knight, it will do no good. Black's King has a flight square.)

168

Here is a variation on the theme of driving away your opponent's King from a key defensive square.

A. White's Queen and Rook cannot mate directly on the back rank because Black has two defenders, the Rook and King. His idea is to drive the King away first, so that it will no longer defend.

B. The White Queen therefore checks, as shown. The Black King must move away toward the corner.

(continued)

Chapter 3

BACK-RANK DEFENSES AND VARIATIONS

Now that you have the basic idea of the back-rank mates, you are ready to explore the subtleties of this theme. In this chapter and the chapters that follow, I will present mating variations and defenses in rapid succession.

TURN THE PAGE AND CONTINUE WITH FRAME 125

166

yes

(The Knight recapture will uncover the checking square for White's remaining Rook. If, instead, the Knight interposes, Rook-takes-Knight will be mate.)

167

Can White mate by first drawing away a Black defender?

☐ yes
☐ no

If he can, draw an arrow to show his key first move.

125

Observe the combination below:

A. White's two Rooks are ready to give check on the same back-rank square, but Black has two defenders. White must get rid of one of these defenders before he can mate.

B. White plays Queen-takes-Rook, giving check.

C. Black's remaining Rook must recapture.

D. Now there are two White Rooks against only one back-rank defender. White moves Rook to Black's back rank, giving check, and mates on the next move.

TURN THE PAGE AND CONTINUE WITH FRAME 126

165

yes
(First the Knight is drawn away, allowing White's Rook to check; then the Bishop interposition is useless.)

166

Can White mate here?

☐ yes

☐ no

If he can, draw an arrow to show White's key first move.

125

NO ANSWER REQUIRED

126

In this position White can begin a back-rank mating combination by first removing one of the Black defenders.

Draw an arrow to show the first move in White's mating sequence:

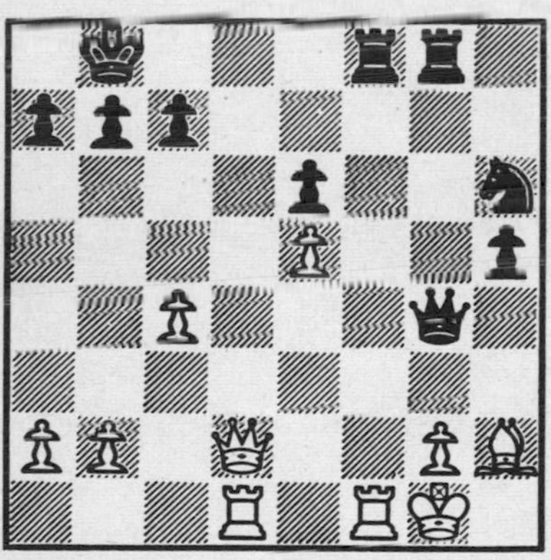

164

no
(Even if Black's Knight is drawn away, Black's Bishop holds the position.)

165

Can White mate by first drawing away a Black defender?

☐ yes
☐ no

If he can, draw an arrow to show his key first move.

126

(When Black recaptures with Rook, White's Queen and Rook have enough power to mate.)

127

Again, draw an arrow to show the first move of White's mating combination:

163

no
(It won't work in positions like this because the Queen will still protect the back rank.)

(After White tries Queen check on the back rank, Black plays Queen-takes-Queen.)

164

Can White mate by first drawing away a Black defender?

☐ yes
☐ no

If he can, draw an arrow to show White's key first move.

127

(When Black plays Rook-takes-Queen, the White Rook check leads to mate.)

128

Here is a position where White can remove one of Black's back-rank defenders, but it does him no good. If Black recaptures with the right piece, it will still be two against two.

If White plays Rook-takes-Rook-check (as shown), how can Black save himself?

☐ by playing Rook-takes-Rook

☐ by playing Queen-takes-Rook

162

(The Black Bishop recapture will allow checkmate by the remaining Rook.)

163

In this next series of frames you will be asked to decide whether White can mate by first drawing away a Black piece.

Can White mate by first drawing away Black's Queen?

- ☐ yes
- ☐ no

If he can, draw an arrow to show White's first move.

128

by playing Queen-takes-Rook
(So it will still be two against two.)

129

In this position, does a White move of Queen-takes-Rook-check (as shown) lead to mate?

☐ yes
☐ no

161

Bishop
(Black must not allow his Knight to be drawn away.)

162

A similar theme.

Draw an arrow to show the first move in White's mating combination:

129

116
(Black's Queen recaptures and maintains guard on the back rank.)

130

If White plays Queen-takes-Queen (as shown), how should Black recapture?

- ☐ with the Bishop
- ☐ with the Rook

160

move A
(And the remaining Rook will deliver the mate after the Knight captures.)

161

Suppose the White Rook checks as shown. Black could only save himself by capturing with his:

- ☐ Bishop
- ☐ Knight

130

with the Rook
(The Rook guards the back rank. Recapture with the Bishop would enable White's Rook to mate.)

131

White has a mating combination, but he must make the key first move. He has several possibilities.

Draw an arrow to show his correct choice:

159

NO ANSWER REQUIRED

160

Which move should White make to begin a mating combination here?

- ☐ move A
- ☐ move B

131

(The correct move, as shown, reduces the number of Black's back-rank defenders from two to one. Then White's Rook can check on the back rank supported by the Pawn. Black must recapture the checking Rook and when White recaptures with the Pawn he makes a new Queen or Rook, giving mate. But not White's Queen takes the other Rook, since Black's Queen can capture and replace the Rook as a guard of the back rank.)

132

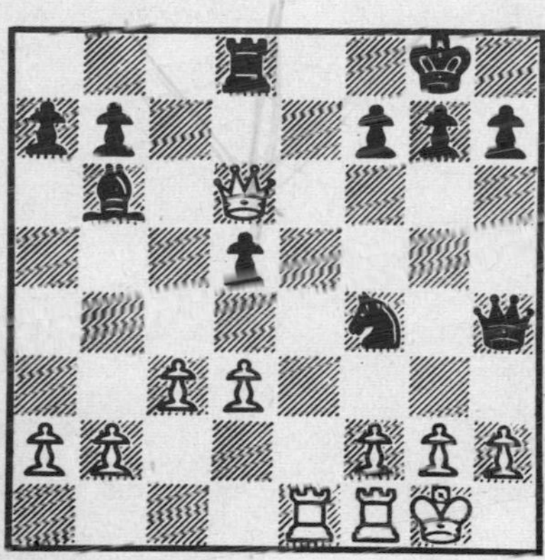

Does a White move of Queen-captures-Rook lead to mate?

☐ yes
☐ no

159

A. Here White has a simple mate. It may be difficult to see at first, since the Black Bishop can capture whichever White Rook checks. Follow the moves for both sides as shown.

B. First the Rook on the left moves down, sacrificing itself. Black's Bishop must capture. (The interposition is useless.)

C. The Black Bishop has captured, and now White's remaining Rook can mate. The idea behind this play is to draw the Black Bishop away from the position from which it guards the key square.

D. Here's what happens if White incorrectly checks first with his other Rook: Now on move two, Rook down threatens mate, but it is not check—so Black has time to defend. As a matter of fact, here he has a very good "defense" by mating White as shown.

132

no
(On Queen-takes-Rook-check, Black's Queen can recapture and guard the back rank.)

133

Does White Rook-takes-Black Rook-check lead to mate in this position?

☐ yes
☐ no

Chapter 4

DISPLACING DEFENDERS

Sometimes a key defensive piece will hinder your attempt to force checkmate. In such situations you may be able to mate after driving that piece away.

TURN THE PAGE AND CONTINUE WITH FRAME 159

133

yes
(White will play Queen-check on Black's back rank after Black recaptures.)

134

Here's a hard one:

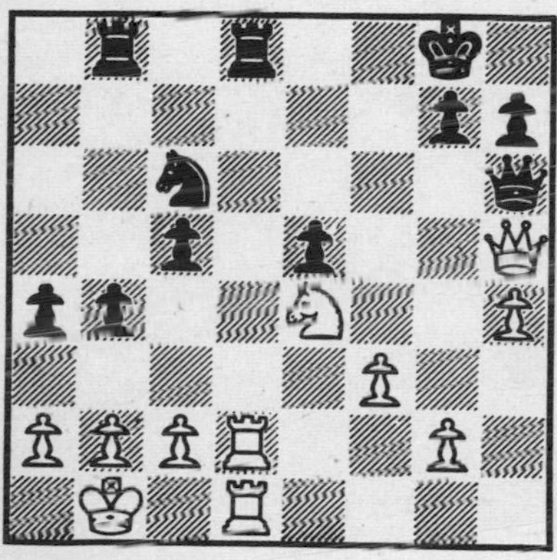

If White plays Rook-takes-Rook-check, can he mate?

☐ yes
☐ no

SUMMARY
Back-Rank Defenses and Variations

In this chapter you were presented not only with more difficult mating combinations, but also with more intricate defenses. You were taught that in some situations power does not work directly, but is effective only if the combination is preceded by a move that eliminates a back-rank defender. You have strengthened your defensive understanding on several points including disconnected Rooks and safe recaptures.

Also, you should be aware of back-rank mating situations not on the back rank, but sideways. As another example, consider the following position which arose in my game with Pilnik (Black) in 1959:

White mates by playing Queen-takes-Knight-check. The King then takes Queen, Rook moves one square to the right, giving mate!

THIS IS THE END OF CHAPTER 3
NOW TURN THE PAGE AND GO ON TO CHAPTER 4

134

yes!
(The mate is finally delivered by the White Queen. Work it out.)

135

Sometimes, you have the choice of making a straight back-rank check or of capturing a defender.

Observe the position below; then, draw an arrow to show the key first move in White's mating combination:

158

NOTE: This is taken from my game with Reshevsky (Black), played in New York, 1962. My opponent has won the United States Championship several times. Actually, I missed this possibility—but I won anyway!)

NOW TURN THE PAGE AND CONTINUE

135

(White can mate by checking directly on the back rank because White's Pawn is supporting the White Queen's checking square. When Black captures White's Queen with his Rook, White can play either Rook-takes-Rook-check or Pawn-takes-Rook [becoming a Queen] -check, and will mate on the next move. Not Queen-takes-Rook-check, which reduces White's power and maintains Black's after Black recaptures with his Rook.)

136

Again, draw an arrow to show White's key first move:

157

White can't mate

158

Here's a back-rank mate sideways!

Draw an arrow showing how White mates:

136

(This capture enables White to reduce Black's power from two to one. White then checks with his Rook, Black captures with his Queen, and White recaptures the Queen with his Pawn, making a Queen or Rook and mating.)

137

Here is a variation on the theme you have just learned.

Observe how White mates:

A. White plays Queen-takes-Rook-check. Black's King must recapture.

B. The Black King has captured White's Queen. And now White's Rook, protected by the Bishop, can mate.

NOW TURN THE PAGE AND CONTINUE WITH FRAME 138

156

White can mate

(. . . followed by Rook mates.)

157

In this position:

☐ White can mate

☐ White can't mate

If he can, show his key first move.

137

NO ANSWER REQUIRED

138

In this and the next few positions, a White sacrifice of Queen-takes-Rook does not lead to mate. You must decide why this is so.

Why does the White move of Queen takes-Rook-check not lead to mate?

- ☐ White does not have enough power.
- ☐ At the end of White's combination, Black has a useful interposition.
- ☐ At the end of White's combination, Black has a flight square.

155

White can't mate
(After White's Queen-takes-Rook-check, Black can defend by playing Queen-takes-Queen. If White tries Queen-takes-Queen, Black must capture with the Rook at the lower left—if Black captures with the Rook next to his King, White will have enough power to mate.)

156

In this position:

☐ White can mate
☐ White can't mate

If he can, show his first key move.

138

White does not have enough power.
(After King-takes-Queen, Black will have Queen and King against two Rooks or two against two, stopping the back-rank mate.)

139

Why does the White move of Queen-takes-Rook-check not lead to mate?

- ☐ White does not have enough power.
- ☐ At the end of White's combination, Black has a useful interposition.
- ☐ At the end of White's combination, Black has a flight square.

154

White can mate
(White reduces Black's back rank defenders, thereby giving himself enough power to mate.)

(The Black Rook will recapture. White will then reply with a Queen check on the back rank.)

155

In this position:

☐ White can mate

☐ White can't mate

If he can, show his key first move.

139

At the end of White's combination, Black has a flight square.

140

This one might seem tricky!

Why does the White move of Queen-takes-Rook-check not lead to mate?

- ☐ White does not have enough power.
- ☐ At the end of White's combination, Black has a useful interposition.
- ☐ At the end of White's combination, Black has a flight square.

153

yes

(It's three against two.)

154

In this position:

☐ White can mate

☐ White can't mate

If he can mate, show his key first move.

140

At the end of White's combination, Black has a useful interposition.
(The Knight capture will uncover the Black Bishop.)

141

Does White have a mating combination beginning with Rook-takes-Rook-check?

☐ yes
☐ no

152

White can't mate
(After the Queen check, Black's Queen interposes.)

153

Can White mate?

☐ yes
☐ no

If he can, show his key first move.

141

yes
(After King-takes-Rook, White mates with his remaining Rook on the back rank.)

142

Before we discuss other mating variations, let's look at some problems for the defender.

White is threatening to play Rook-takes-Rook, followed by mate. It's Black's move. Surprisingly enough, he has only one good defense:

- ☐ Rook takes Rook, as shown
- ☐ Pawn advances one or two squares, as shown

151

yes

(The Queen sacrifice will be followed by Rook mate on Black's back rank.)

152

In this position:

☐ White can mate

☐ White can't mate

If he can, show his key first move.

142

Pawn advances one or two squares, as shown
(If Black plays Rook-takes-Rook, he gets mated. Or if Black moves his unpinned Rook one square, for example, White plays Rook-takes-Rook-check and mates with the other Rook. Advancing the Pawn to create a fleeing square is Black's only defense.)

143

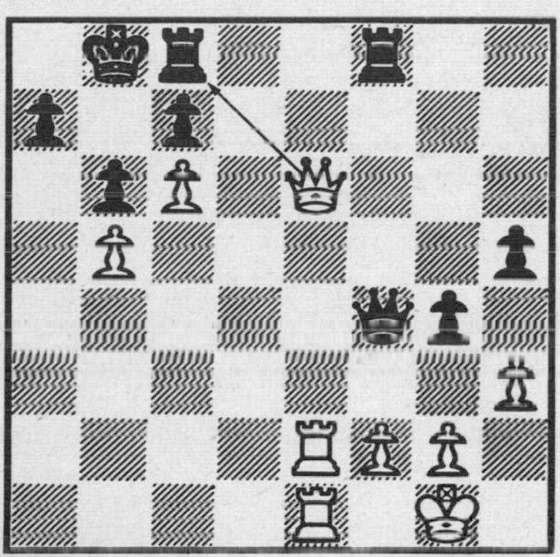

Suppose that White plays Queen-takes-Rook-check (as shown).

Black's only saving move is to recapture with:

- ☐ his King
- ☐ his Rook

150

151

Now you will be asked to decide whether or not White has one of the back-rank mating combinations you have learned.

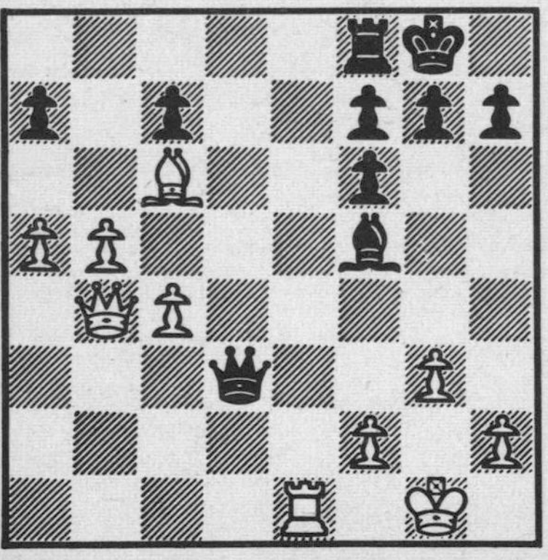

Can White force mate?

☐ yes

☐ no

If he can, draw an arrow to show his key first move.

143

his Rook
(Black would be mated if he captured with his King: the White Rook checks, Rook-takes-Rook, Rook-takes-Rook-mate.)

144

Here is one of the most critical of all the back-rank defenses. The following positions will show you the idea:

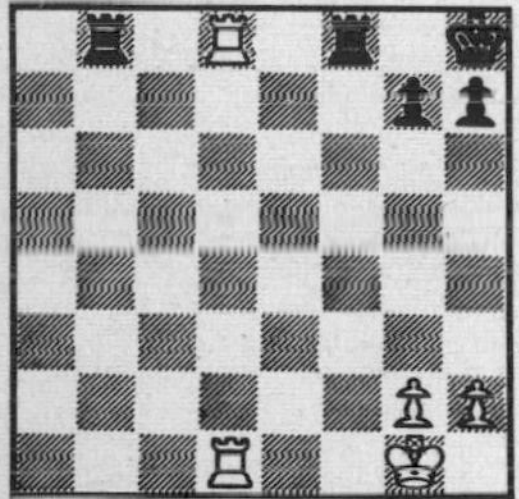

A. Surprisingly enough, in this position White cannot mate, no matter which Rook he takes. Even though they seem disconnected, the Rooks protect each other!

B. But in this position, if it is White's move, he has an easy mate.

(continued)

149

(The King capture would lead to mate after Rook checks.)

150

Draw an arrow to show Black's saving defense:

144 (continued)

C. Then how does Black defend in positions such as this one? He cannot play Rook-takes-Queen, but he can play Rook interposes (as shown).

TURN THE PAGE AND CONTINUE WITH FRAME 145

148

(The Rook capture protects the back rank.)

149

Draw an arrow to show Black's defense:

144

NO ANSWER REQUIRED

145

Draw an arrow to show how Black saves himself from checkmate:

147

148

This one is a little different. Draw an arrow to show Black's correct defense:

145

(The only defense.)

146

Draw an arrow to show Black's correct defense:

FOR THE CORRECT ANSWER TO FRAME 146, TURN THE PAGE AND THEN TURN THE BOOK AROUND

146

(Capture by the other Rook would leave one defender of the back rank to two attackers.)

147

Draw the usual arrow to show Black's saving shot: